KARL & CLAIR

Are You MORE
Spiritual
Than a 5th Grader?

A father and his 5 daughter share the
timeless teachings of Morris Venden

Pacific Press®
Publishing Association

Nampa, Idaho | Oshawa, Ontario, Canada
www.pacificpress.com

Cover design by Gerald Lee Monks
Cover design resources from the authors
Inside photos provided by the authors
Inside design by Kristin Hansen-Mellish

The authors assume full responsibility for the accuracy of all facts and quotations as cited in this book.

Unless otherwise noted, all scripture quotations are from the HOLY BIBLE, NEW INTERNATIONAL VERSION®. Copyright © 1973, 1978, 1984, 2011 by Biblica, Inc.® Used by permission. All rights reserved worldwide.

Scripture quotations marked KJV are from the King James Version.

Scripture quotations from *The Message*. Copyright © by Eugene H. Peterson, 1993, 1994, 1995, 1996, 2000, 2001, 2002. Used by permission of NavPress Publishing Group.

Scriptures marked NCV quoted from The Holy Bible, New Century Version, copyright © 1987, 1988, 1991 by Word Publishing, a division of Thomas Nelson, Inc. Used by permission.

Scriptures quoted from NKJV are from The New King James Version, copyright © 1979, 1980, 1982, Thomas Nelson, Inc., Publishers.

Scripture quotations marked NLT are taken from the Holy Bible, New Living Translation, copyright © 1996, 2004, 2007. Used by permission of Tyndale House Publishers, Inc., Carol Stream, Illinois 60188. All rights reserved.

Scriptures quoted from NLV are from The NEW LIFE Version, copyright © 1969, 1976, 1978, 1983, 1986. Christian Literature International, Canby, OR 97013. Used by permission.

Scriptures quoted from Phillips are from J. B. Phillips: The New Testament in Modern English, Revised Edition, copyright © J. B. Phillips 1958, 1960, 1972. Used by permission of Macmillan Publishing Co., Inc.

Scriptures quoted from TEV are from the Good News Bible—Old Testament: Copyright © American Bible Society 1976, 1992; New Testament: Copyright © American Bible Society 1966, 1971, 1976, 1992

Scriptures quoted from *The Voice* are from *The Voice Bible*, copyright © 2012 Thomas Nelson, Inc. The Voice™ translation © 2012 Ecclesia Bible Society All rights reserved.

Additional copies of this book are available by calling toll-free 1-800-765-6955 or by visiting http://www.adventistbookcenter.com.

ISBN 13: 978-0-8163-5082-7
ISBN 10: 0-8163-5082-5

13 14 15 16 17 • 5 4 3 2 1

DEDICATION
To Lee and Marji Venden

Not only do you teach that it's all about Jesus, you live it. Obviously, this book never could have happened without your enthusiastic and encouraging endorsement. From the brainstorming to the bookshelf, you have been unbelievably magnanimous in your support of this project. We are deeply indebted and thankful to you. What an invaluable gift of grace you are in our lives!

With heartfelt love in Christ,

Karl and Claire

MUCHO THANKS TO:

Raj Attiken, the most passionate person I know who preaches and lives the gospel.

Alex Bryan, whose friendship and influence keeps bringing me back to Jesus.

Japhet De Oliveira, whose invitation to participate in the OneProject has been a game changer for me.

Bill Gravestock, for kindly sharing your parable of "The Everlasting Gospel and Ben Trying."

Lloyd Grolimund, a bright beacon of righteousness by faith that shines around the world.

Ron Klein, my doctor and friend who takes every opportunity to share the teachings of Morris Venden.

Jon and Lisa Larrabee, who graciously loaned me their island to write this book.

LaDonna LaVenture, the consummate face of grace every time I see her.

Shona Macomber, a brilliant artist, teacher, and friend who was most helpful with our art class in this book.

Fred and Mary Kaye Manchur, treasured friends who have been so supportive and encouraging in life's journey.

Jarrod and Heidi McNaughton, "Hello . . ." You make me happier than the color yellow.

Dwight Nelson, for your friendship, your teachings, your support, and your quote in this project.

Leo Ranzolin and Laffit Cortes, whose invitation to present these themes at Pacific Union College was just the impetus I needed to make this book happen.

Richard and Bec Reid, beautiful people who are sold-out followers of Jesus.

Brett and Holly Spenst, for the golf and art lessons.

The Team: Clive, Dan, Desi, Elliot, Hazel, Hollie, Jakin, Jerry Mahn, Jerry Taylor, Kasper, and Kay. It's a great blessing to serve Jesus with you.

MY FAVORITE PREACHER

My favorite preacher wasn't preaching anymore. His voice had been silenced by the archenemy, and for several years, my voice had been silent about why that was the case. The weapon used to take him out was a form of dementia known as Pick's Disease, or FTD. FTD is a rare neurodegenerative disease that causes progressive destruction of nerve cells in the brain, leaving its victim incapable of experiencing meaningful relationships or avoiding inappropriate behaviors.

The irony was hard to miss. There seems something deliberate behind a neurosurgeon acquiring Parkinson's Disease, or Beethoven losing his hearing. Hell purposefully attacked my father in a way that clearly related to the two primary focuses of his ministry:

1. A meaningful, personal relationship with Jesus is the sum and substance of the Christian life.
2. An ongoing, personal relationship with Jesus will transform flawed human beings into His likeness.

Viewing the effects of FTD in my father, without understanding their source, could cause some to question the legitimacy of the message of salvation by faith in Christ alone. For years, I refrained from speaking about Dad's symptoms, fearful that some might wrongfully conclude his message was impotent.

Then, during the summer of 2006, I sat across a dinner table from Karl Haffner. We were both guest presenters at a camp meeting in North Carolina. As we ate our meal, Karl asked about my dad. He seemed genuinely interested, and that day I found myself telling him things I had refrained from disclosing to so many who appeared casually curious. The cafeteria emptied and I lost track of time as the afternoon wore on. Karl listened intently as my heart released some of its sorrow and sadness. And then I saw the tears begin trickling down his cheeks. They didn't stop for some time, as he told me how much my father's ministry had meant to him. In the years since, my heart has been often warmed by the memory of that conversation and Karl's caring.

Earlier this year, someone told me about a California symposium where Karl presented for a weekend in the very church Dad had pastored for eight years. His theme was "Keeping the Voice of Morris Venden Alive," and his message was the same two-strings-on-the-violin that Dad had played for nearly fifty years.

On more than one occasion, my father said to me, "I'm not a great preacher, but I have a great message!" That message was always Jesus. Only Jesus. Ever Jesus. I thank God for adding Karl's voice and pen to the symphony, and giving him the same violin to play. I know my dad would be pleased. I'm certain Jesus is!

Lee Venden

In Memory

Elder Morris L. Venden, the widely known and much loved Seventh-day Adventist preacher, passed to his death on February 10, 2013. He was eighty years old and had struggled with frontotemporal dementia (FTD).

In Elder Venden's memory, a portion of the proceeds from this book will be donated to the Association for Frontotemporal Degeneration, a nonprofit organization whose mission is the following:

- Promote and fund research into finding the cause of FTD, and therapies and cures for FTD.
- Provide information, education, and support to persons diagnosed with an FTD disorder and for their families and caregivers.
- Educate physicians and allied health professionals about FTD and how to improve patient care.
- Bring about greater public awareness of the nature and prevalence of FTD and the needs of those who are coping with it.
- Advocate with public officials and promote public and private programs that provide appropriate, affordable, and high-quality, long-term health care and social services.
- Facilitate the international exchange of ideas regarding FTD.

For more information, visit http://www.theaftd.org.

TABLE OF CONTENTS

Author's Note

This book is a repackaging of a Week of Prayer that Morris Venden conducted at Andrews University. (To hear Elder Venden preach the original series, visit http://pacificpress.com/MoreSpiritualThan5thGrader.) If you listen to the sermons, you will recognize that much of the material in this book comes from that week. For the most part, I have not attributed the quotes directly to Elder Venden, and I have freely tweaked his wording in an effort to make his sermons more readable. To begin, however, I am quoting directly a few paragraphs that were so central to Elder Venden's messages.

During that week, Elder Venden offered this disclaimer about Weeks of Prayer:

> There's a great deal of misunderstanding about conversion. I think most young people have had the impression that conversion is a sudden, overnight change, so that you are completely different, and you have no problems. Or if you have problems for very long afterwards, you just simply weren't converted.
>
> And so, this is one of the reasons why many young people become disenchanted with Weeks of Prayer. We took some surveys of the impact that Weeks of Prayer had had on a large cross section of young people. The Weeks of Prayer were down near the bottom of the list, and I got to investigating as to why, and here's the reason why: they had the idea that it's sort of a spring and fall cleaning. And usually they seem to have a sense of some sort of emotional pitch building up to some sort of crescendo, and they wake up the week after . . . and realize that things are still the same. They thought that they had really had something happen to them, but things are still the same. And so, all you can do, at best, is to wait for another Week of Prayer.
>
> I'm not interested in a Week of Prayer this week, really, in the traditional sense. I hope this week that we can have the tools clearly at hand so that we can have a Week of Prayer next week, and the week after, and the one after that, until Jesus comes. And if we can't have that kind of week, then it's going to be a loss, let's face it.[1]

Elder Venden then concluded the week by reiterating this point:

I'm not interested in some kind of big pitch here this morning; all the things you are never going to do again. No, the only kind of decision that is worth a dime is deciding that you are going to join Mary at the feet of Jesus—today, tomorrow, and the next day, and the next day until Jesus comes. I am asking you for that kind of decision, so that you can have a Week of Prayer next week.[2]

Now I am presenting Elder Venden's sermons and ideas for Weeks of Prayer around the world. My prayer is for this book to be a reminder and a resource during the long seasons that follow a Week of Prayer. To this end, I have included practical guidelines in the appendixes to help you nurture an ongoing, consistent friendship with Jesus. In my mind, nothing is more important for an authentic spiritual life.

My favorite quote from Elder's Venden's Week of Prayer articulates this well:

The devotional life in the experience of the Christian is not optional. Thousands of people have the idea that it is a nice thing to do. Why, you know, if you have some time, read the Bible, pray; it will make God feel good. And there are some people we feel are kind of geared that way, you know, the mystics. They are the ones that can sense the presence of God and practice the presence of God. But me? No way! It just doesn't work that way. So I'll try something else. *There is nothing else to try.*

If you, as a Christian, haven't yet discovered meaning in the personal, daily devotional life, fellowship with Jesus, don't try anything else. There is nothing else to try. There is nothing else. And it is not optional any more than lack of communication with my wife is optional. It is the entire basis of the Christian experience—ongoing communion and fellowship with Jesus. . . .

I want to point out to you today and this week before we are finished that the only thing we can do to become, and remain, Christians is to know this fellowship, this relationship. That's all. That's all! And it is the gospel that is wonderfully simple and simply wonderful.[3]

ENDNOTES

1. Morris L. Venden, "Knowing for Sure," sermon delivered November 10, 1975, Andrews University, Berrien Springs, MI.

2. Morris L. Venden, "How Jesus Lived," sermon delivered November 14, 1975, Andrews University, Berrien Springs, Michigan.

3. Morris L. Venden, "Knowing for Sure," sermon delivered November 10, 1975, Andrews University, Berrien Springs, MI.

PREFACE

KEEPING VENDEN'S VOICE ALIVE

When I was in fifth grade, I owned a Tonka truckload of sermon tapes. Really. As a kid, my heroes included preachers such as Charles Bradford, Roland Hegstad, Henry Wright, E. E. Cleveland, and Floyd Bresee. But my favorite cassettes featured the rich, baritone voice of Pastor Morrie Venden. (OK, so I wasn't your typical kid!)

I mainlined Morrie's messages. Then, I often escaped to the basement with my dad's big, black Bible, and, with the aid of a clothesbasket that served as my pulpit, I impersonated this man that I knew only by his voice—and his theology. To this day, I credit Pastor Venden as one of the most influential people in my faith journey.

I am not alone. There are many, especially in the Seventh-day Adventist tradition, who point to Pastor Venden as the life-transforming voice of righteousness by faith alone. Wikipedia describes him as "a 'master' of the art of preaching amongst Adventists. Tapes of his sermons have been distributed widely. . . . Venden was a strong advocate of both justification and sanctification by faith alone."[1]

When we started writing this book, my daughter Claire was in fifth grade. She, too, has a keen interest in spiritual matters. She always has. In the flyleaf of her Bible that I read to her at bedtime, I wrote this letter:

> My Dearest Claire,
> "In the beginning" is where we started. "Amen. Even so, come, Lord Jesus. The grace of the Lord Jesus Christ be with you all. Amen" is where we ended. In the 1,480 pages in between, we listened to God speak.
> We started with one bookmark. By Leviticus, we had six bookmarks. By Chronicles, you declared yourself a bona fide bookmark collector, and the stack of bookmarks were as thick as the Psalms. But by the New Testament, you had lost interest in the collection, and we were back to one Post-it note stuck to the chapter we'd read next.
> We began when you were just five years old. "Daddy, read me the Bible," you'd beg every night at bedtime. So I'd lay your boxed

lampshade on its side to direct the light so I could read "the lamp unto our path." Early on, I'd read until you'd drift to sleep. Since some of the stories in Judges are rated PG-13, I was thankful you were snoozing. By Ecclesiastes, you'd no longer fall asleep. Sometimes I thought you were asleep, so I'd finish reading the chapter and close the Bible. Just then, one little finger would poke out from under the covers signaling a "one." Then your sleepy little voice would pine, "One more chapter, Daddy. Please, just one more chapter." By the New Testament, you didn't need to say anything—the finger said it all. So I'd read one more chapter. Sometimes we'd repeat that routine a dozen times until I'd say, "No more. Go to sleep."

You've changed in our journey through the Bible. You're taller. You can read for yourself now. And your spiritual attunement has matured as well. Your spirit was a sponge through this journey, often interrupting me with questions that clued me in that you were absorbing every word.

"Why did Athaliah kill the royal family?" you asked me in 2 Kings. You loved the story of Obadiah hiding the hundred prophets from Jezebel (1 Kings 18); you loved it so much you insisted that I read it again and again. And you had more than a few questions when the bears mauled the forty-two kids who mocked Elisha for being bald (2 Kings 2). That story didn't put you to sleep. You were mesmerized with the story of Jotham, Abimelech, and the talking trees (Judges 9).

Our goal was not to limit our reading to the pretty parts of Scripture; rather, we chose to read it all—the good, the bad, and the boring. (Remember the book of Numbers with pages and pages of names that I couldn't pronounce?) Some stories made me chuckle; other passages caused *me* to doze; then there were moments of tearful moisture when I just came undone by the outrageous grace of God and the overpowering pleasure I felt when I'd gaze at your perfect face on the pillow.

Claire, nothing brings me greater joy than to be called your daddy. I was filled with pride when your kindergarten teacher's husband shared how your teacher told him of the many students she has taught through the years, you stand out in her mind as a kid with extraordinary spiritual depth and heart. She remembers you well as a kid who passionately loved Jesus. I pray you will keep growing in Jesus. I know you are crazy in love with Him and that He feels the same about you. May that friendship deepen every day.

Thank you, Claire, for going through God's Word with me. I treasure the times we shared with our heavenly Father. If His love for us is anything like my love for you, then truly "neither height nor depth, nor anything else in all creation, will [compromise that love]" (Romans 8:39).

I value you more than life. I love you more than words. I praise God for you more than always.

Your Daddy

Ironically, the kindergarten teacher who remembered Claire as deeply interested in spiritual matters was Morrie Venden's daughter-in-law, Marjorie Venden. Not surprisingly, Claire has always held a special fondness for Mrs. Venden. So when Marjorie and her husband, Lee, recently visited our church in Ohio to present an All About Jesus seminar, Claire was delighted to reunite with her favorite kindergarten teacher.

It was at this seminar that Lee slipped me a priceless gift—a CD collection of twenty of his father's best sermons. "It was after my dad shared these sermons," Lee explained, "that revival broke out in the churches and campuses where he had preached. Forty years later, people still talk about the outpouring of God's Spirit following these messages. I think these are the most Spirit-anointed sermons he ever preached."

Dwight Nelson, who has served as the senior pastor for more than thirty years in the very church where Pastor Venden shared the Week of Spiritual Emphasis that is foundational to this book, reflects on when he was a student: "I was a sophomore in college when Morris Venden came to campus for our spring Week of Prayer. Yes, I was a multigenerationed Adventist kid, weaned on the great truths of our community of faith. But it took Pastor Venden's conversational preaching and teaching about a relationship with Jesus to cast the vision of a daily devotional walk with Him. I'm still on that walk with the same Jesus. And I still thank God for sending Morrie Venden when I needed Him."

I could have scarcely anticipated the visceral impact the sermons would have on me—again. Sermon after sermon after sermon, I devoured Morrie's timeless presentations of righteousness by faith. It felt like a time machine had transported me back to the fifth grade. The dormant stories were reawakened in my soul, and a tsunami of God's Spirit flooded over me. Along the way, there were tears, giggles, memories, insights, prayers, and divine encounters aplenty.

"I can't get enough of those sermons," I said to Lee. "Your dad's singular focus on a relationship with Jesus is like a geyser of fresh water in a drought of legalism and spiritual despondency. I can't even tell you how life changing the sermons have been. His theology is so profound, and yet my daughter understands it."

Thus, the seed was planted for this book. Brainstorming together, Lee and Marjorie enthusiastically endorsed the idea of me teaming up with Claire and repackaging Morrie's classic messages. "Old theology for a new generation," was the idea. Or, "new theology for an old generation that has forgotten." Actually, we figured, it would be both.

So I approached Claire. "Would you like to write a book with me? All you have to do is listen to some sermons on your iPod and then write down your thoughts. You can help others to see God through your eyeglasses as a fifth-grader."

Reluctantly, she said, "I don't know, Dad."

"You might get paid for every book that sells."

"I don't care," she shrugged.

"And you could sign books with me."

"So?"

"Well, you'd be doing a big favor for Mrs. Venden."

"Really?"

At last, I had found her soft spot. That night Claire started listening to the first sermon. Lights out, Morrie's soothing voice flowing through the stereo, when Mom popped her head into the room and asked, "Claire, are you asleep yet?"

"*Ssh!*" came the curt reply. "I'm working!"

So at the end of each chapter, you're invited to join Claire and me in the classroom where we'll break down the chapter into five courses:

- **FIRST-GRADE ART:** The chapter in a picture.
- **SECOND-GRADE COMPUTERS:** The core learning expressed via technology.
- **THIRD-GRADE BIBLE:** A verse to commit to memory (along with a paraphrase).
- **FOURTH-GRADE WRITING:** A quote or reflection that captures the main teaching.
- **FIFTH-GRADE MATH:** The lesson reduced to an equation or two.

This book is the record of our journey together through a series of sermons that I think are every bit as relevant today as they were when Richard Nixon was the president; every bit as relevant as when a fledgling new community of faith called Seventh-day Adventists emerged with a renewed emphasis on the ancient truth of righteousness by faith. To that young church, grappling to understand the doctrine foundational to all other teachings, Ellen White wrote, "The thought that the righteousness of Christ is imputed to us, not because of any merit on our part, but as a free gift from God, is a precious thought. The enemy of God and man is not willing that this truth should be clearly presented; for he knows that if the people receive it fully, his power will be broken."[2]

Morris Venden presented this truth of Christ's righteousness in a powerful and winsome way at the 1975 fall Week of Spiritual Emphasis at Andrews University. His sermons that week were all included on the disk that Lee gave me. While Claire and I have updated some details and added a few chapters of our own, we are profoundly indebted to Pastor Venden for his ideas that shape this book. The stories, the theology, and, in many cases, the very words belong to Morrie— although specific notations are not cited in most cases. This is our attempt to preserve Pastor Venden's legacy and keep his voice alive.

Morris Venden devoted his career to helping others receive this "precious thought" of righteousness as a free gift from God. The more deeply we understand this, the more robust and vibrant our spirituality will be. So join us as we explore together this life-transforming doctrine of faith. Perhaps, together, we can graduate to the fifth grade.

ENDNOTES —————————————————————————————

1. Wikipedia contributors, "Morris Venden," Wikipedia, accessed October 21, 2013, http://en.wikipedia.org/wiki/Morris_Venden.

2. Ellen G. White, *Gospel Workers* (Washington, DC: Review and Herald® Publishing Association), 161.

- 1 -

GOD IN A BOX

In West Africa, the locals have preserved the legend of the sky maiden. According to the tale, there was a tribe that was greatly blessed. The people owned cattle and orchards and gardens and vineyards in great abundance. In time, however, tribal members noticed that their lands and cows were yielding less and less. This baffled them. The harder they worked, the less they harvested.

Determined to solve the mystery, one young warrior stayed up all night spying on the cattle. What happened next stunned him. His eyes widened in disbelief as he beheld the scene unfolding before him.

A gorgeous young woman holding a large empty bucket sailed down on a moonbeam. She milked the cows and then returned in the same manner in which she had come.

Determined to catch the culprit, the warrior set a trap the following evening. When he had the woman cornered, he demanded an explanation.

"Please," she cowered, "I mean you no harm. It's just that my people are starving, and the only thing that is keeping them alive is the milk I deliver from your cows." Crumpled at his feet, she begged, "Please let me go."

"I will let you go, under one condition," the warrior said. "You must marry me."

"I will marry you," she replied, "if you will allow me three days to return to my homeland to gather my possessions and say farewell to my people."

The request seemed reasonable, so an agreement was made.

Three days later, the woman returned, carrying a large box. "I will be your wife and make you very happy," she told him. "But there is one more condition."

"And what is that?" he wondered.

"You must promise never to look inside this box."

Well, it seemed like an easy enough commitment to keep, so the two were married. And they lived happily, but not ever after.

One day, while his wife was out, the man could stand it no longer. He had to know what was in that box. So he opened it.

He couldn't believe what he saw.

When the woman came back, she knew intuitively that something was different. Something had changed in her husband. She confronted him, "You looked in the box, didn't you?"

"Well, um, OK," he stammered. "Yes! I looked in your silly little box."

The woman frowned in disapproval.

Feeling defensive, he continued, "I don't know what the big deal is. Maybe you don't even know this," his voice escalated into a high-pitched squeal, "but your box is empty! There is nothing in it!"

"I must leave you," the woman stated matter-of-factly.

"What?" Now he was incredulous. "You are going to leave me because I looked inside an empty box?"

"Oh, no," she explained. "I'm not leaving you because you opened the box. I thought you probably would. I'm leaving you because you said it was empty. It isn't empty; rather, it contains what I hold most dear to my heart. It is full of the sky and light and air and the smells of my home in the sky. When I went home for the last time, I filled that box with everything that is most precious to me to remind me of where I come from. How can I be your wife if you see what I value most as emptiness?"

With that, she disappeared and never returned. Such is the legend of the sky maiden.

My Box

As you open this book, know that it contains what I treasure most, which is to say, what I would put in my box. Without hesitation, I would fill that box with my *faith*. But what, then, belongs in my box?

If you were to package your faith, what would you put in your box? Perhaps you'd include a book such as the Bible or the Koran or *The Great Controversy*. After all, such books contain truth, right? Would not a holy book be an apt symbol of faith?

Or maybe you'd fill your box with tofu, because religion should be healthy (and tasteless), correct? Or what about a replica of a church building? How about theological position papers pounding gays?

For me, such symbols do not accurately capture what I would consider to be the core of faith. For many, however, faith or religion is synonymous with a tome of truth or a list of behaviors to embrace or shun. Just look at the definition of *religion* at Dictionary.com: Religion is "a specific fundamental set of *beliefs and practices* generally agreed upon by a number of persons or sects: the Christian religion; the Buddhist religion" (emphasis added).

"Beliefs and practices"—box them up, and you've got the guts of faith. Or should there be more? Surely, some folk understand religion to be twenty-eight fundamental beliefs neatly packaged between book covers. Others might choose twenty-eight fundamental practices, such as going to church, paying tithe, ripping on carnivores (God have mercy on vegetarians who eat people!), and so on. No wonder people peek into the box of faith and say it's empty. If faith is nothing more than internal beliefs or external behaviors, then I understand why some find it to be a vacuum of meaninglessness.

Religion as Behavior

Digging a little deeper, defining faith or religion in terms of behavior colors one's understanding of sin. Using this construct, sin equals bad behavior. Eating cheese, killing your neighbor's cat, stealing towels from a hotel, lying about reading the "terms and conditions" before surfing a Web site, tearing the tag off a mattress—these behaviors, along with a zillion other indiscretions, can blotch the Christian's portfolio of perfection. Who isn't guilty of sinful behavior?

Jesus touched on the core of faith and the nature of sin in His classic story of the prodigal son. Remember the story? A wealthy father has two sons. The younger kid squanders his dad's inheritance on prostitutes, parties, and pot. He lands in a pigpen with mud and manure oozing through his toes. That's when he dares to imagine that his father might forgive him for his sin. But notice in the story how he understands sin. His understanding parallels his brother's definition of sin.

"When he came to his senses, he said, 'How many of my father's hired servants have food to spare, and here I am starving to death! I will set out and go back to my father and say to him: Father, I have *sinned* against heaven and against you. I am no longer worthy to be called your son; make me like one of your hired servants' " (Luke 15:17–19; emphasis added).

He plans to confess, "I have sinned." How had he sinned? Bad behaviors. He was a naughty boy.

Back to the story: "So he got up and went to his father. But while he was still a long way off, his father saw him and was filled with compassion for him; he ran to his son, threw his arms around him and kissed him. The son said to him, 'Father, I have sinned against heaven and against you. I am no longer worthy to be called your son' " (verses 20, 21).

The kid executes his plan and says, "I have sinned." In this mind-set, religion is all about what we do and what we don't do.

I've seen this mind-set in my own denomination. At the 2010 General Conference Session in Atlanta, more than seventy thousand Seventh-day Adventists convened to conduct church business. Midweek I decided to change hotels to get a little closer to the convention center.

At check-in, I asked the woman behind the desk, "You busy this week?"

"Oh, yes," she exclaimed. "We're completely booked up. It's all because of some convention this week with a church—Seventh-day Witnesses or something like that."

"Oh? Interesting," I replied.

"Yeah," she said, "they are really into witnessing! A lot of them keep giving me this book." She pulled out a copy of *The Great Controversy.* "Like I would ever read this!" she hissed sarcastically. "But I guess this is what they believe—it's in this book." With a sigh, she said, "The upside to this group is that we never have to refill our coffee urn. I think coffee is forbidden by their religion."

I didn't have the heart to tell her that I am a Seventh-day Adventist. Ask her about my church, however, and she would probably refer you to *The Great Controversy.* Or she would talk about shunning coffee. In other words, she would describe a behavioral model of faith that is all about what we believe and what we do. Beliefs and practices, right?

RELIGION AS RELATIONSHIP

Surely faith is more than just a cold set of beliefs and practices, don't you think? I believe the essence of faith, or religion, is not about *behaving for* God; it is about *being with* God. We see this in the father's response to the rebellious son.

> "But the father said to his servants, 'Quick! Bring the best robe and put it on him. Put a ring on his finger and sandals on his feet. Bring the fattened calf and kill it. Let's have a feast and celebrate. For this son of mine was dead and is alive again; he was lost and is found.' So they began to celebrate.
> "Meanwhile, the older son was in the field. When he came near the house, he heard music and dancing. So he called one of the servants and asked him what was going on. 'Your brother has come,' he replied, 'and your father has killed the fattened calf because he has him back safe and sound' " (verses 22–27).

Funny, isn't it, how the father makes no mention of pot, parties, or prostitutes? He never alludes to the boy's bad behavior. See, the father understands faith in a different way—different from the younger son, and different from the older son as well.

The father's love is for the person, unconditional of the performance. His love is there regardless of good or bad behavior. Such love is hard to comprehend.

Once at a high school assembly, I shared a story that illustrates our heavenly Father's unconditional love. I was shocked at the students' reaction.

In my story, it seems a young fellow was driving home from school when he snagged his fender on the bumper of another car. He was on the verge of tears, because the car was his dad's prized possession, fresh out of the showroom. How was he ever going to explain the damage to his dad?

The driver of the other car was sympathetic, but explained that they must exchange registration and insurance information. As the young man was digging through the glove box, a piece of paper fell out. In his dad's distinctive scrawl were these words: "In case of an accident . . . remember, son, it's you I love, not the Buick!"

To my chagrin, the students heckled me. "No way! That could never happen!" Another shouted, "That's not my dad." "Nice fairy tale, preacher!" They couldn't comprehend love so extravagant—so, well, untethered to behavior.

Back to the text:

> "The older brother became angry and refused to go in. So his father went out and pleaded with him. But he answered his father, 'Look! All these years I've been slaving for you and never disobeyed your orders. Yet you never gave me even a young goat so I could celebrate with my friends. But when this son of yours who has squandered your property with prostitutes comes home, you kill the fattened calf for him!' " (verses 28–30).

The older brother felt superior because he had modeled exemplary behavior, while his brother had behaved very badly. In his mind, he deserved better treatment because he never sinned. That is, he never chased the parties, pot, or prostitutes.

Notice the father's response: " 'My son,' the father said, 'you are always with me, and everything I have is yours. But we had to celebrate and be glad, because this brother of yours was dead and is alive again; he was lost and is found' " (verses 31, 32).

The father doesn't excuse the younger kid's bad behavior, but he was not upset about it either. His concern was about a relationship. So he throws the robe on his son's back, reinstating him into the family. He puts the ring on his finger, symbolizing a reconciled relationship. He tells the older brother, "You never left me; our relationship was never in jeopardy, so what's your issue?" The father's concern was not with bad behavior. It was all about the broken relationship.

As a father, I get it. When my daughter Lindsey was born, I never tired of marveling at our miracle. I gazed into her ice-blue eyes and entertained Papa thoughts: *She's a lot cuter than most infants, probably a future Miss America. She is so gifted at putting her hands in her mouth, probably a future dentist. She sure prattles a lot without saying anything, probably a future politician (or preacher?).* Soon my wife demanded I get out of the crib and go back to work.

The thought of leaving Lindsey smacked of cruel and unusual punishment. So I struck a deal: "I'll take Lindsey to the church office with me, and you can sleep." Mom was happy. Dad was happy. And Lindsey? She was so happy she was foaming at the mouth. Our *Brady Bunch* joy, however, was short lived.

At the office, I laid Lindsey on my desk and turned to make a phone call. During the call, I twirled around to admire my daughter. That's when I discovered she had been raptured. My first thought was, *How did she dash off when she can't walk? She's a future Olympic sprinter!*

Then the error of my assessment hit me like a gavel. She didn't *dash* off the desk. She *fell* off the desk. As in *plunged* three feet to an unyielding cement floor covered in carpet the thickness of paper. I was so wrong. *She'll not be an Olympic sprinter at all. More likely a diver.*

Slamming down the phone, I raced around the desk to behold my princess sucking up all the air in King County so she could express herself. In that split second of silence, I dared to imagine that maybe she hadn't noticed the tumble. Then came the shriek that removed all doubt—and half of my permanent hearing.

I scooped her up and begged her forgiveness. "I'm *soooooooo* sorry," I cried. "*Ooooh,* sweetie, Daddy's sorry. I didn't mean to, I should've put . . . I wasn't watching . . . I didn't know you could fall . . . Daddy will give you anything . . . unlimited trips to Disneyland, my firstborn—oh wait, you *are* my firstborn." Her convulsing body and tears the size of jellyfish didn't ease my guilt.

I called 9-1-1. Then a pediatrician. Then Mom. All parties assured me no permanent damage was done. So I held my sobbing sweetheart and rocked her gently. But I couldn't stop shaking or crying.

Now how would you think of me as a father if my next move had been to give Lindsey a good old-fashioned whipping for what she had done? Suppose I scolded her: "What were you thinking, you little delinquent? (Slap!) At three weeks old, you're old enough to know better than to fall off a desk. (Smack!) Just wait till your mother gets home. (Spank!)"

Chances are, you can't imagine a dad so demonic. And neither can I.

Yet how many of us paint our heavenly Father with such insane notions? As if God were peering over our shoulders, ready to fry us when we fall, like a judge waiting to bust us, with the electric chair plugged in.

No. No. No! God is a Father who aches when His children ache. He hurts when we hurt. He grieves when we fall. He's not poised with a switch to punish the sin; rather, He's bending with arms open to embrace the sinner. To the Father, sin is not about falling; it is about falling *away from Him.* Big difference. Sin is not about doing bad things; it's about living outside of God's presence.

This idea is so fundamental to faith, let me repeat it. *Sin is not a bad behavior, it is a broken relationship.* Christian faith, then, is not behaving for God; it is *being with* God.

The Practice of Religion

But what about the practice of faith? Isn't there something the Christian should *do*? Yes! But the behavior God expects from us is this: to remain in His presence.

Nicholas "Nick" Herman discovered this truth. He served in the military and then worked for a while in transportation. But he felt deeply dissatisfied. He worried chronically about whether he was saved.

His spiritual breakthrough came while observing a tree. It occurred to him that for a tree to flourish, it must remain deeply rooted in something other than itself. In that moment, Nick unmasked the mystery of spiritual life. The words of Jesus took on new meaning: "Remain in me, as I also remain in you. No branch can bear fruit by itself; it must remain in the vine. Neither can you bear fruit unless you remain in me. I am the vine; you are the branches. If you remain in me and I in you, you will bear much fruit; apart from me you can do nothing" (John 15:4, 5).

In the shadow of that tree, Nick decided to use the rest of his life as an experiment that he called the practice of a "habitual, silent, secret conversation of the soul with God." He would focus solely on "remaining" in Jesus, rooted in Christ.

Nick remained very obscure. Eventually, he got a job washing dishes in a kitchen. But the people around him found that rivers of living water flowed out of him that made them want to know God the way he did. One coworker wrote of Nick, "The good brother found God everywhere, as much while he was repairing shoes as while he was praying with the Community."[1]

After Nick died, his friends compiled a book of his letters and conversations. Apart from the Bible, that book is thought to be the most widely read book of the last four centuries. This unknown dishwasher has sold more copies of his book than John Grisham, Tom Clancy, and J. K. Rowling have sold of their books combined.

Today we know Nick as Brother Lawrence, and his book as *The Practice of the Presence of God.* He writes, "There is not in the world a kind of life more sweet and delightful than that of continual conversation with God. Those only can comprehend it who practice and experience it; yet I do not advise you to do it from that motive. It is not pleasure which we ought to seek in this exercise; but let us do it from a principle of love, and because God would have us."[2]

That's the most important thing in life. That's what I would put in my box—a friendship with Jesus. Herein is the core of Christian faith: finding constant pleasure in His divine company.

THE CLASSROOM

FIRST-GRADE ART

SECOND-GRADE COMPUTERS

Last week when Dad and I were taking a walk, I tried to explain to him how to get more "likes" from his pictures on Instagram. I said, "Dad, your pictures are boring and predictable. They are all of buildings or barns or mountains. Post a picture of us instead. It doesn't have to be a perfect picture—just something of people." So right then, I snapped and posted a picture of us (right) and immediately got more than forty likes! I tried to tell Dad it's all about people and relationships, not places and buildings. The same is true when it comes to faith. It's all about a relationship with Jesus, not colorful stained glass or a church building. When will my dad learn?

THIRD-GRADE BIBLE

"The God who made the world

and everything in it, this Master of sky and land, doesn't live in custom-made shrines or need the human race to run errands for him, as if he couldn't take care of himself. He makes the creatures; the creatures don't make him. Starting from scratch, he made the entire human race and made the earth hospitable, with plenty of time and space for living so we could seek after God, and not just grope around in the dark but actually find him. He doesn't play hide-and-seek with us. He's not remote; he's near. We live and move in him, can't get away from him!" (Acts 17:24–28, *The Message*).

"The God who created us doesn't need servants to fetch Him a glass of lemonade or go wash His car. He's a big boy. He can take care of Himself. After all, He made us. We didn't craft the Creator. He made the whole world for no other reason than to be with us. And this isn't a cosmic game of hide-and-seek where we shall never find Him. Oh no! Everywhere we turn He is right there—desperately wanting to be found" (Acts 17:24–28, our paraphrase).

FOURTH-GRADE WRITING
In this chapter, I learned that the most important thing about being a Christian is faith. Faith isn't about behaving (going to church, not smoking, etc.) or your beliefs (saying you are a Christian or saying you believe in it); it's about having a relationship with God. A relationship with Jesus, I think, means you love Him. And that's basically it.

FIFTH GRADE MATH
Faith ≠ Behavior
Faith ≠ Beliefs
Faith = Being with God

ENDNOTES

1. *The Practice of the Presence of God,* quoted in Jerry C. Lee, "Practice of the Presence, 2," *The Night Watches* (blog), accessed August 15, 2013 http://thenightwatches.wordpress .com/tag/quotes/.

2. "Gail Sanders, "Eight Quotes From *The Practice of the Presence of God* by Brother Lawrence," Yahoo Voices, accessed July 12, 2013, http://voices.yahoo.com/eight-quotes -practice-presence-of-7241692.html.

- 2 -

WHEN GOD GAGS

With the title of his book, *And Are We Yet Alive?* Bishop Richard Wilke confronts his denomination with a sobering question. He writes,

> Our sickness is more serious than we at first suspected. We are in trouble, you and I, and our United Methodist Church. We thought we were just drifting, like a sailboat on a dreamy day. Instead, we are wasting away like a leukemia victim when the blood transfusions no longer work. Once we were a Wesleyan revival, full of enthusiasm, fired by the Spirit running the race set before us like a sprinter trying to win the prize. Circuit riders raced over hill and valley. New churches were established in every hamlet. Our missionaries encircled the globe. Now we are tired, listless, fueled only by the nostalgia of former days, walking with a droop, eyes on the ground, discouraged, putting one foot ahead of the other like a tired old man who remembers, but who can no longer perform.[1]

Of course, Wilke is talking only about the Methodist Church, right? Or should other churches be included in his indictment? I wonder, Are we, Christ's church of today, yet alive? Or are we Laodicea—a listless, lifeless, lukewarm body?

Morris Venden launched his 1975 Week of Spiritual Emphasis with a teaching about Laodicea—the troubled, end-time church. Listen to how John the revelator describes it:

> "To the angel of the church in Laodicea write:
> "These are the words of the Amen, the faithful and true witness, the ruler of God's creation. I know your deeds, that you are neither cold nor hot. I wish you were either one or the other! So, because you are lukewarm—neither hot nor cold—I am about to spit you out of my mouth. You say, 'I am rich; I have acquired wealth and do not need a thing.' But you do not realize that you are wretched,

pitiful, poor, blind and naked. I counsel you to buy from me gold refined in the fire, so you can become rich; and white clothes to wear, so you can cover your shameful nakedness; and salve to put on your eyes, so you can see.

"Those whom I love I rebuke and discipline. So be earnest and repent. Here I am! I stand at the door and knock. If anyone hears my voice and opens the door, I will come in and eat with that person, and they with me" (Revelation 3:14–20).

What is most tragic about this church is that it does not know its condition. Apparently, it is possible for people to believe they are justified, rich, and in need of nothing and yet be "wretched, pitiful, poor, blind and naked."

Nobody makes any progress until they face the truth about their condition. You must admit your wretched helplessness.

This church called Laodicea is lukewarm. What makes something lukewarm? Well, go to your kitchen sink and turn on the hot water on the left and the cold water on the right. Excuse me for the elementary lesson in home economics, but if you want lukewarm, you turn on equal parts of hot and cold. Lukewarm is the combination of hot and cold.

Now let's return to Laodicea. So are we to understand, then, that a Christian is hot on the left side and cold on the right side? Hot on the top, cold on the bottom? Is it similar to my wife's ultrasound results of Claire before she was born, when the doctor said, "I'm guessing 80 percent girl, 20 percent boy?" (I pictured a freakish baby that was Karl Jr. in the head, with a body belonging to Karla!) What does it mean that we are lukewarm, neither hot nor cold?

Consider the statement that Jesus made about the church leaders in His day: "Woe to you, teachers of the law and Pharisees, you hypocrites! You clean the outside of the cup and dish, but inside they are full of greed and self-indulgence" (Matthew 23:25). Here we find a clue as to what makes a person lukewarm—cold on the inside and hot on the outside. Outside, Jesus says, you appear beautiful; inside you're full of dead men's bones. That's lukewarm. Doing all the right things for all the wrong reasons. Going through all the right motions with all the wrong motives.

This hypocrisy makes God sick. He says, "You make me want to vomit" (Revelation 3:16, *The Message*). So why does God have a gag reflex toward His people in the last days? The text offers a couple of reasons.

A SPIRIT OF SELF-SUFFICIENCY

First, God is repulsed by a spirit of self-sufficiency. This is the prideful heart that says, "I don't need You, God. I can do it on my own. I'm big enough. I'm strong enough. I'm smart enough. I don't need to depend on the Holy Spirit. I don't need to surrender. I don't need to fall on my knees in humility. I don't need accountability. I don't need any help. I'm good enough to save myself."

I know that attitude of self-sufficiency. Recently, I hurried into a meeting, failing to turn off my headlights. Eight hours later, the battery was dead. Of course, this was not a dire emergency. After all, there were dozens of people leaving the office who could help me jump-start the car. In fact, I was parked right next to a car that belonged to a friend who was a member of my church. He would have been happy to help. But I couldn't bring myself to ask.

Instead, I pushed the car by myself, trying to build sufficient speed for a jump-start. All the while, I carefully eyed the front door of the building, hoping nobody would notice my predicament. I managed to push the car a block or so down the driveway. But whenever someone rolled by, I quickly jumped in my car (parked precariously in the middle of the road) and pretended to talk on my cell phone. I waved the drivers by; and when the coast was clear, I resumed my futile attempts to coax life into the car. Finally, I gave up and called AAA. Before AAA came, however, I managed to get the car rolling again; this time it sputtered to life. And most important, nobody ever knew I needed help.

When God sees this attitude of self-reliance in His children, He says, "I want to throw up."

If any city in the ancient world flaunted its independence and self-sufficiency, it was Laodicea. Strategically located at the intersection of three major highways, it was a hub of wealth and excess. Traders from Europe to the Middle East or Africa all sojourned through the Lycus Valley and Laodicea. Because of the advanced Roman highway system and the *Pax Romana* (the Roman peace), Laodicea was a lucrative nucleus of commerce and economic opportunities. The city enjoyed greater prosperity by far than did any of the other seven churches addressed in Revelation.

Moreover, the Laodiceans were ambitious folk. They set the standard for the avant-garde. They dreamed big. Thus, in A.D. 26, they submitted a bid to build a temple for Tiberius. In our day, this would be similar to a city bidding to host the Olympics or the Super Bowl. Focusing a global spotlight on the city would result in heightened prestige and windfalls of cash. When Rome passed on Laodicea's bid, the civic leaders hissed, "All right Rome, we'll show you!"

Sure enough, over the next thirty years, they pulled off an economic coup. The proliferation of wealth in their city was unprecedented. In A.D. 60, there was a massive earthquake in Laodicea. When the Roman government offered financial assistance (like FEMA today—only faster), the leaders in Laodicea basically said to Nero, "No thanks, we don't need you or your money. Now, how do *you* like being rejected?" The Roman historian Tacitus describes the event like this: "One of the famous cities of Asia, Laodicea, was that same year overthrown by an earthquake, and, without any relief from us, recovered itself by its own resources."[2]

Laodicea had a town motto. Similarly, in our day, many cities boast a slogan or a motto. New York City is the "City That Never Sleeps." Cedar Bluff, Alabama, is the "Crappie Capital of the World." Knik, Alaska, prides itself as the "Dog-Mushing Center of the World." Berkeley, California, is also known as

"Berzerkeley." If you're looking for the "Horseradish Capital of the World," go to Tulelake, California. The "Richest Square Mile on Earth" hails from Central City, Colorado. If you're keen on fruitcake, then you should visit a therapist, but I digress. Actually, Corsicana, Texas, is the town known as the "Fruit Cake Capital of the World." And Phoenix, Oregon, wears the label "The Other Phoenix."

I grew up in Minot, North Dakota, where the welcome sign asks, "Why not, Minot?" (Having lived there, I could generate a very long list of answers to that question!) For fifteen years, I lived in Walla Walla, Washington—the "Town So Nice, They Named It Twice!" And currently, I reside in Dayton, Ohio, the "Birthplace of Aviation." (Yep, the Wright Brothers invented the airplane at their bicycle shop in Dayton, not Kitty Hawk.)

So now for Laodicea's motto: "I am rich. I have acquired wealth. I do not need a thing." This was the well-known slogan that captured the essence of the townspeople there.

Laodicea led the way in textile technology and cultural trends. They were the innovators of very expensive black wool. This proved to be a hot export item. Fashionistas all over the Roman Empire ordered their togas (a smoking-hot item in that day) from Laodicea.

Laodicea was also famous for its educational center that featured a prestigious, cutting-edge medical school. The physicians were pioneers in the field of ophthalmology. The most-famous doctor in town was Demosthenes Philalethes, who authored one of the most influential ophthalmological works of antiquity, the *Ophthalmicus*. Historians speculate that he may have been the first person to develop medicines to treat eye disorders. This salve came from Phrygian powder and was exported around the world. Ancient coins featured images of Laodicean doctors from that era. They were pioneering leaders in applying the high-tech solutions of their day to the field of health care.

So Laodicea's stock kept climbing north. The city enjoyed great affluence and influence. It had the best technology, health care, and education. It did not need FEMA. Not even a major earthquake could slow it down. And in the center of all this awesomeness sat a church that reflected the same spirit of self-sufficiency and pride. "We are rich. We have acquired wealth. We don't need a thing. Isn't God lucky to have us on His side?"

And God gags.

The Spirit explains, "Hey, church at Laodicea. You don't understand your true condition." It's interesting that the Spirit does not say, "You have so much that is positive. Just remember to stay humble." Instead, the Spirit rebukes this church as "wretched, pitiful, poor, blind and naked."

Ouch!

A SPIRIT OF APATHY

Another dynamic that repulses God has to do with the church's apathy and lukewarm spirit toward the needs of others. Some context and historical background helps us understand the metaphor of lukewarm water.

Six miles to the north of Laodicea was the city of Hierapolis. World famous for its hot springs and spa treatments, Hierapolis attracted people from around the world who came in search of relaxation and healing. Wikipedia adds, "The great baths were constructed with huge stone blocks without the use of cement and consisted of various closed or open sections linked together. There are deep niches in the inner section, including the bath, library, gymnasium."[3]

To the south and a little east of Laodicea was the town of Colossae. Paul's letter to the residents of Colossae includes four references to Laodicea. Colossae was best known for its ice-cold underground springs, which bubbled up to offer thirsty people the best drinking water around. It controlled the Perrier or Evian water of the day.

Laodicea was positioned between the hot springs and the cool springs. They did have potable water there, but it was hard and brackish. Remember, the Laodiceans had seemingly unlimited resources and a fierce sense of self-sufficiency. So they built aqueducts up to Hierapolis and down to Colossae to pipe in their water. The problem was that by the time the water flowed into Laodicea, the hot water wasn't hot, and the cold water wasn't cold.

Of what value then was their tepid water? This was a sore spot that stung their civic pride. "Hey, Laodicea," outsiders would mock, "your water stinks!" So the residents of Laodicea would have connected immediately to the judgment of Jesus, "You are neither cold nor hot."

A big part of the judgment against Laodicea centers on its indifference, its lukewarm attitude. In his classic book *The Screwtape Letters,* C. S. Lewis describes a briefing that the devil gives his nephew, Wormwood, on the techniques of tempting people. The goal, the devil says, is not overt evil but indifference. The devil instructs Wormwood to keep the person cozy and snug above everything else. If the person starts to think of things with eternal significance, then encourage him to think about lunch or anything else. And then comes this definitive job description: "I, the devil, will always see to it that there are bad people. Your job, my dear Wormwood, is to provide me with the people who do not care."

That's the evil one's strategy: produce lukewarm Christians who are neither hot nor cold, people who don't care. There's an old story of a newly hired young preacher standing at the window of his study, crying. He was looking out at a scene of busy people scurrying here and there. He saw dope peddlers, prostitutes, junkies, panhandlers, and thieves. One of the church members came near, gently placed a hand on his shoulder, and said, "Don't worry. After you've been here a while, you'll get used to it."

"Yes, I know," the minister replied. "That's why I am crying."

It happens almost imperceptibly, newbies in Christ, hot for His cause, grow apathetic. Not cold and anti-God, just lukewarm.

Anne Ortlund remembers her childhood when she and her friends would play church. In her book *Up With Worship,* she writes,

> We'd get the chairs into rows, fight over who'd be preacher, vigorously lead the hymn singing, and generally have a great carnal time. The aggressive kids naturally wanted to be up front, directing or preaching. The quieter ones were content to sit and be entertained by the up-fronters.
>
> Occasionally we'd get mesmerized by a true sensationalistic crowd-swayer—like the girl who said, "Boo! I'm the Holy Ghost!" But in general, if the up-fronters were pretty good they could hold their audience quite a while. If they weren't so good, eventually the kids would drift off to play something else—like jump rope or jacks.
>
> Now that generation has grown up, but most of them haven't changed too much. Every Sunday they still play church. They line up in rows for the entertainment. If it's pretty good, their church may grow. If it's not too hot, eventually they'll drift off to play something else—like yachting or wife swapping.[4]

It's easy to get lulled into a state of being lukewarm, right? To lose contact with Christ. To fuss over churchy stuff that doesn't amount to a hill of used Communion cups. To settle into my good works and somehow hope that'll get me into heaven some day.

If your spiritual life is lukewarm these days, take heart. Jesus offers this guidance: "I counsel you to buy from me gold refined in the fire, so you can become rich; and white clothes to wear, so you can cover your shameful nakedness; and salve to put on your eyes, so you can see" (Revelation 3:18).

Morris Venden asserts that in the end it always comes back to the righteousness of Jesus. His gold addresses our bankrupt souls. His robe covers our shameful wickedness. His salve opens our blind eyes.

What the Laodicea church needs is the experience of righteousness by faith. And when that kind of message begins to get through to Laodicea, it shakes up the church.

Why would anyone get shaken when they hear of Christ's righteousness? This message would be startling for those who rely on something else for their spirituality. It would shake the foundation of their good works right out from under them, and they would be exposed—naked and wanting.

Jesus says, "I stand at the door and knock" (verse 20). I don't want to be down in the basement when Jesus knocks. I don't want to be out in the kitchen stuffing my face. I don't want to be sleeping in the bedroom. I don't want to be in the family room playing video games.

In other words, I don't want to be so preoccupied in all my self-sufficiency and all my spiritual competencies that I miss the knock. Nor do I want to be apathetic and miss this grand adventure of an intimate friendship with Jesus.

When Jesus knocks, I'd like to hear Him, wouldn't you? I'd like to open the door and let Him in. He's not pushy; He only knocks. But He says, "If anyone hears my voice and opens the door, I will come in and eat with that person, and they with me" (verse 20).

Stop. Listen. And you will hear Him knocking right now.

The only remedy for a lukewarm spirit of self-sufficiency and apathy is to foster a friendship with Jesus.

So He knocks patiently, longingly, persistently. Open that door, and Jesus will fill your empty space.

In the *Chicago Tribune Magazine,* actor Kyle Chandler was asked a series of finish-the-sentence questions. One question was, "I'd give anything to meet _____."

Chandler answered, "God Almighty. I'd like to share my favorite meal with him, and I'd let him do all the talking."[5]

This offer is open to Chandler—and to you.

THE CLASSROOM

FIRST-GRADE ART

SECOND-GRADE COMPUTERS

 Jesus follows u on Twitter. He wants 2 b ur bff. Any #followers?

THIRD-GRADE BIBLE

"Look! I stand at the door and knock. If you hear my voice and open the door, I will come in, and we will share a meal together as friends" (Revelation 3:20, NLT).

"Knock, knock."

"Who's there?"

"Jesus."

"Jesus who?"

"Jesus Christ."

"Oh! Really? And what do You want?"

"Well, I'd like to come in and hang out with you. Have dinner. Talk. No big agenda—let's just be friends."

Knock, knock.

Knock, knock.

"I'm still here. Knocking" (Revelation 3:20, our paraphrase).

FOURTH-GRADE WRITING

What makes God throw up? Two attitudes: (1) Self-sufficiency; (2) Apathy:

1. "I don't need . . ."
   - God
   - church
   - prayer
   - devotions
   - Scripture

2. "I don't care . . ."
   - about the poor
   - about the dope peddlers, prostitutes, junkies, panhandlers, and thieves
   - about the newborns in faith
   - about the condition of my soul
   - about the One knocking at the door

FIFTH-GRADE MATH

$X + Y = Z$

(Code: X = Hot; Y = Cold; Z = Laodicea)

Here's the chapter expressed in another equation:

$B \div (S)(A) = \neg\, GF$

(Code: B = Believer; S = Self-sufficiency; A = Apathy; $\neg$ = Not; GF = Genuine Follower)

ENDNOTES

1. Richard Wilke, *And Are We Yet Alive?* (Nashville, TN: Abingdon Press, 1986), 9, quoted in David J. Riggs, Oak Ridge Church, accessed February 24, 2013,

http://oakridgechurch.com/riggs/1c15-58c.htm.

2. Tacitus, *The Annals,* trans. Alfred Church, ed. Moses Hadas, Modern Library Classics (New York: Modern Library, 2003), http://www.sacred-texts.com/cla/tac/a14020.htm.

3. Wikipedia contributors, "Hierapolis," Wikipedia, accessed October 22, 2013, http://en.wikipedia.org/wiki/Hierapolis.

4. Anne Ortland, "Playing Church," Sermons Illustrated November/December 1988 at http://www.biblestudytools.com/pastor-resources/illustrations/progress-of-church-11548548.html (accessed October 30, 2013).

5. Cheryl Lavin, "Kyle Chandler," Fast Track, *Chicago Tribune,* March 18, 2001, accessed August 16, 2013 http://articles.chicagotribune.com/2001-03-18/features/0103180515_1_heroes-evangelists-russian-movie.

– 3 –

"A QUARTERBACK AND A COACH WENT TO THE TEMPLE TO PRAY"

Whether you paint your face and go shirtless to every game of your favorite football team or you could care less, you probably know about two of the more talked about names surrounding the sport.

The first is Tim Tebow. When he took over as quarterback for the ailing Denver Broncos, suddenly they started winning. It wasn't just the wins; it was *how* they were winning. Week after week, Tebow orchestrated these impossible, last-second, come-from-behind, dramatic miracles. Statisticians have crunched the numbers and have figured that the odds of anybody pulling off what Tebow did are about one in twenty-seven million! No wonder he is dubbed "the miracle man."

The title also refers to the fact that Tim Tebow is a very outspoken, devout Christian. In fact, his very name has become synonymous with praying. "Tebow-ing" in our vernacular today means praying.

Sports Illustrated columnist Rick Reilly figured nobody could be that squeaky clean, so he tried to dig up some dirt on Tebow. However, instead of exposing a scandal, he learned things about Tebow that the public didn't know. Reilly tells of Tebow's ritual before every game:

> Every week, Tebow picks out someone who is suffering, or who is dying, or who is injured. He flies these people and their families to the game, rents them a car, puts them up in a nice hotel, buys them dinner (usually at a Dave & Buster's), gets them and their families pregame passes, visits with them just before kickoff(!), gets them 30-yard-line tickets down low, visits with them after the game (sometimes for an hour), has them walk him to his car, and sends them off with a basket of gifts.
>
> Home or road, win or lose, hero or goat.[1]

How can you not love this guy? Everyone loves Tim Tebow—especially Claire. At the height of his popularity, I would often regale the family with the latest Tebow story at our dinner table.

"I heard on the news today that Tim Tebow is raising over a million dollars to build a children's hospital."

"Did you know that Tim Tebow has publicly pledged to keep himself pure until he gets married?"

"Tebow was born to missionary parents in the Philippines. And he was home-schooled."

Almost every night, I had a new story. As far as role models go, I am thankful for Tim Tebow. I can't think of a better professional athlete for my kid to emulate. So as you read the rest of this chapter, please keep this in mind: *I am Tim Tebow's biggest fan.*

The other name that has hogged the football headlines is Jerry Sandusky. He is the former assistant coach at Penn State University who was found guilty on forty-five of forty-eight charges of molesting boys. I still remember when the story broke. Just seeing his face triggered a visceral impulse to throw a lamp at the TV. Nothing raises my ire more than accounts of grown men abusing boys for their own prurient pleasure. I understand why many people say, "Jerry Sandusky is a scumbag. I hate that man."

Two More Men

Now keep those two men in mind as we consider the story of two more men. The parable is found in Luke 18:9–14.

First, notice to whom Jesus was speaking: "to some who were confident of their own righteousness and looked down on everyone else" (verse 9). Luke identifies two attributes: (1) self-righteousness, and (2) condescension toward others.

Now when it comes to being self-righteous and having a condescending and judgmental spirit, we are dealing with a problem that is really hard to self-diagnose. For twenty-five years, I have seen a steady stream of people parade through my office and confess sins that are destructive. "Pastor," someone says, "you've got to help me with my mismanaged anger, because it's destroying my family." Or, "Pastor, my eating disorder is killing me. Help!" Or, "Pastor, my compulsive pornography addiction is undermining my marriage."

But I have never had anyone say, "Pastor, you have got to help me with my spiritual conceit. I am so quick to condemn people. I am self-righteous and judgmental and condescending of others. Please help me! My spiritual arrogance is sabotaging my soul and destroying my relationship with God."

Now, it's true that self-righteousness and looking down on others is fatal, but we don't see it in ourselves. There is no twelve-step program for the spiritually smug.

So to crack this mask of self-sufficiency, Jesus told this parable: "Two men went up to the temple to pray, one a Pharisee and the other a tax collector" (verse 10).

THE PHARISEE

First, we are introduced to the Pharisee. "The Pharisee stood by himself and prayed: 'God, I thank you that I am not like other people—robbers, evildoers, adulterers—or even like this tax collector. I fast twice a week and give a tenth of all I get' " (verses 11, 12).

Have you ever heard somebody praying, presumably to God, but it's obvious that they are really talking to someone within earshot? "God, forgive my husband (who is listening right now) for selfishly forgetting our anniversary, and tell him that all is forgiven if he picks up that gift for me that You know is on layaway right now at Macy's."

Frank Schaeffer, the son of Francis and Edith Schaeffer, founders of the fundamentalist community L'Abri in Switzerland, has written a memoir titled *Crazy for God: How I Grew Up as One of the Elect, Helped Found the Religious Right, and Lived to Take All (or Almost All) of It Back*. As the title suggests, Frank is quite cynical regarding matters of faith. In the book, he describes his mother's prayers. He writes,

> Mom sometimes would hold forth in prayer for—literally!—[hours]. . . .
> . . . When prayed out loud, the prayers were often a not-so-subtle vehicle for sermons. These sermons (masquerading as prayer) were for the good of those here on earth who were eavesdropping on what was purporting to be a conversation with God but was really a way to say things to Dad, that Mom didn't dare say out loud, or a way for Dad or Mom to preach to an unbeliever.
> Praying out loud was also a way of advancing one's case, the advantage being that no one dared interrupt you or argue back. . . .
> I sometimes wondered if God ever tried to duck out of the room when he saw Mom coming.

Likewise, I wonder if God tried to duck out of the temple when He saw this Pharisee coming. The Pharisee is not praying to God at all; he's broadcasting his goodness.

His prayer is an unmasked recital of his righteousness. "God, I thank you that I am not like other people—robbers, evildoers, adulterers—or even like this tax collector" (verse 11).

He is so judgmental, this man. It's a good thing we're not like that, right? Or at least, we're a lot more discreet and refined in our judgmental barbs.

The other day I hit the drive-through at Taco Bell and ordered a couple of tacos (beans instead of beef, in case you are judging me). Only after I placed my order did I see the newest menu item—the Cantina Burrito. Only heaven knows why I fall for any "new" menu item at Taco Bell, because let's face it, *everything* served at Taco Bell contains the same ingredients. Instead of putting the cheese on the beans, they come out with a "revolutionary, new burrito" by putting beans on the cheese—and then charge an extra buck for the innovation. So don't ask me why I fell for this marketing scam, but I did. I yelled at the speaker: "Can I change my order? Make that one taco, and I'll try your new Veggie Cantina Burrito."

The guy said, "OK, no problem." But then he left his transmitter on, enabling me to hear the ensuing dialogue that he had with the girl preparing the food. This gave me the opportunity to exercise my primary spiritual gift—eavesdropping. And since I'm using this story in a book, I think my taco qualifies as a tax deduction!

So when the guy told this girl to change my order, she was incredulous. "He changed his order? What an idiot! Why did you let the idiot change his order?"

The guy defended me. "Don't judge him," he said. "Your job is not to judge. Your job is to make burritos."

Again, she reiterated, "The guy is an idiot."

Then her coworker said something you don't expect to hear at a drive-through. "Don't judge the guy," he said firmly. "Only God can judge."

That'll preach! I thought. *Only God can judge.*

Imagine if our churches modeled this kind of nonjudgmental love. Our Lady of Lourdes Catholic Church in Daytona, Florida, attempts to live out this expression of nonjudgmental love. In its bulletin, you'll find this welcome to visitors:

> We extend a special welcome to those who are single, married, divorced, gay, filthy rich, dirt poor, yo no hablo Ingles. We extend a special welcome to those who are crying newborns, skinny as a rail, or could afford to lose a few pounds. We welcome you if you can sing like Andrea Bocelli or like our pastor who can't carry a note in a bucket. You're welcome here if you're "just browsing," just woke up or just got out of jail. We don't care if you're more Catholic than the Pope, or haven't been in church since little Joey's baptism.
>
> We extend a special welcome to those who are over sixty but not grown up yet, and to teenagers who are growing up too fast. We welcome soccer moms, NASCAR dads, starving artists, tree-huggers, latte-sippers, vegetarians, junk-food eaters. We welcome those who are in recovery or still addicted. We welcome you if you're having problems or you're down in the dumps or if you don't like "organized religion." We've been there too.
>
> If you blew all your offering money at the dog track, you're welcome here. We offer a special welcome to those who think the earth is flat, work too hard, don't work, can't spell, or are here because grandma is in town and wanted to go to church.
>
> We welcome those who are inked, pierced—or both. We offer

a special welcome to those who could use a prayer right now, had religion shoved down their throat as a kid or got lost in traffic and wound up here by mistake. We welcome tourists, seekers and doubters, bleeding hearts . . . and you![2]

Imagine if our churches threw down a welcome mat like that. I suspect people would be trampling over each other to get in. Instead, I fear that this Pharisee's attitude is more the norm. We're thankful that our churches are safe harbors from the "bad guys."

The Pharisee continues his prayer informing God, "I fast twice a week and give a tenth of all I get" (verse 12). His claims are quite loaded. Everyone listening to Jesus would have noted the man's righteousness. According to Leviticus 23, an Israelite was required by the law to fast only once a year during the Day of Atonement. This guy fasts *twice a week*—a hundred times more than what the law requires!

Then he says that he gives "a tenth of *all* I get" (Luke 18:12; emphasis added). Don't skim over the little word *all*. According to Old Testament law, farmers would have already tithed on commodities like wine, grain, or oil. So it wasn't necessary to pay an additional tithe on such items. But this guy goes ahead and tithes on *everything*—above and beyond the minimum required.

Other items did not require a tithe. For example, one rabbinic teaching said the people were not required to tithe on celery. Celery is one of those negative-calorie foods where it takes more energy to digest it than is in the food itself. I ask you, Of what value is celery? Why do we even bother with the stalk? It's not a real food like M&Ms or Fig Newtons or gluten burgers. Apparently, God doesn't like celery either!

So this Pharisee is doing serious extra credit work. He assumes that he can enhance his status in the eyes of God by all of his religious activities. He is so blind, this man, that he doesn't even see how obnoxiously self-absorbed he is. He prays to God, but really it's just a recitation of his works, his devotion, and his righteousness. "Me, me, me"—that's the tenor of his prayer.

Ever met somebody like that? Some time ago, my wife and I went to lunch with a church administrator from another state. The whole meal he kept name-dropping. "I'm friends with this church leader, and I know so and so, and me, I, me, mine, myself, I'm . . ." It was suffocating. The most painful part was how clueless he was to his narcissistic air.

On our drive home, I said to Cherié, "It was nauseating how controlling and careful he was to make the conversation only about him." Then I had this unsettling thought, and I asked her, "Do I ever do that?"

Silence.

"Well," she finally said, "you may want to talk to a trusted friend about that."

So I did. The next week, I was having lunch with Oprah . . .

Not really! I just made up that whole story. But should the ugly truth get told, the tale *is* based on a true story. The Pharisee's cancer of spiritual narcissism poisons my soul too. No doubt, the disease is more—way more—pervasive than I even know.

Now, it's critical to understand that at this point in the story, everybody listening in Jesus' day would have felt very favorable toward the Pharisee. Since we already know the punch line and we know of the larger body of work with respect to the Pharisees, we do not naturally side with the religious guy. We are repulsed by his arrogance and self-righteousness; when Jesus told the story, this was not so. Back then, everybody would have venerated the Pharisee. He was holy, generous, committed. The listeners did not scorn him nor find him repulsive. He was the Tim Tebow of their day. In our day, we are not offended by Tebow's generous life, nor should we be. He is a great man of God.

THE TAX COLLECTOR

Enter the tax collector. He was the Jerry Sandusky of the day. Nobody felt fuzzy, warm feelings toward this guy. The mere mention of his name would have triggered an indignant outrage from the crowd.

No rabbi in the ancient world—other than Jesus—ever told a story that positioned a tax collector as the hero. Just his name knotted stomachs and wrinkled foreheads, pointed fingers and hurried heartbeats.

Jesus continued, "But the tax collector stood at a distance. He would not even look up to heaven, but beat his breast and said, 'God, have mercy on me, a sinner' " (verse 13).

The text says that both men separated themselves but for very different reasons. The tax collector "beat his breast." The act of beating one's chest was considered an expression of extreme agony in that culture; it was very rare. This gesture is mentioned only twice in Scripture—once here, and the other time when Jesus is crucified at Golgotha.

Listen to the tax collector's simple prayer: "God, have mercy on me, a sinner" (verse 13). There is no long list of good deeds here. His prayer is short, stark, and dark.

The tax collector understands his utter and absolute spiritual depravity. He has no delusion that he deserves anything from a just and holy God. Absent are any claims of piety. Silenced are any boasts of godly bravado. There is no hint of entitlement in his prayer.

And now it gets personal.

Is there any Pharisee heresy in your heart? Do you feel a tinge of pleasure when you're the first to hear about the head elder's arrest for drunk driving? (Assuming you're not the head elder.) Ever find yourself scowling in judgment against the single mom who can't control her kids in church? Any scent of spiritual smugness when the pastor gets busted for sleeping in the wrong bed?

What's scary to me is how firmly lodged this Pharisee is in me, and I don't even see him. He enjoys a long-term lease, and I can't even admit that he lives in my neighborhood. My judgmental, jaded heart is worse than whatever sin I see in others, and I don't even know it. I have such a corrupt heart. This is what Jesus was trying to expose in His story.

Jeremiah 17:9 says it well: "The heart is deceitful above all things, and desperately wicked; who can know it?" (NKJV). We see the evil in others with blinding clarity while we are clearly blind to the evil polluting our own hearts.

The very best acts of righteousness performed by the Pharisee or Tim Tebow or you or me—the best we can offer amounts to a mountain of used rags. The very best works that we can offer flow out of corrupt hearts with selfish, insidious, dark, and twisted motives.

The best you've got is garbage. You can be impeccably orthodox and doctrinally pure right down to your decaffeinated, nonalcoholic, smoke-free, vegan, home-schooled, little soul—but you're no less a wretched sinner in need of God's grace.

Somehow, I'm tempted to think that because I've never molested a kid or murdered an enemy or cheated on my wife that my sins aren't so bad. So I'm inclined to believe that God is getting a good deal with me—like when God paid it all on Calvary for me, He got a refund. Surely God's impressed with my commitment, isn't He? After all, I'm a card-carrying ASI, GYC, NAD, SDA.

God have MERCY.

Here's the inconvenient reality of grace: God loves Jerry Sandusky every bit as much as He loves Tim Tebow. There is nothing that Tim Tebow has done that has earned him favor in God's sight, and there is nothing that Jerry Sandusky has done that has disqualified him from heaven. It's not fair. And it's terribly unsettling. But it's true. And it's grace.

Jerry Bridges put it this way: "Your worst days are never so bad that you're beyond the reach of God's grace. And your best days are never so good that you're beyond the need of God's grace."[3] Put another way: "Your Sandusky days are never so bad that you're beyond the *reach* of God's grace. And your Tebow days are never so good that you're beyond the *need* of God's grace."

The good news in all of this is that God can love even a hardened, self-righteous, judgmental, elder brother Pharisee like me. Morris Venden shared this insight when he underscored the words of Jesus: "Those whom I love I rebuke and discipline" (Revelation 3:19). That sounds strange at first, and yet when Jesus rebukes and chastens, He has tears in His voice.

In Matthew 23, we find one of the most hard-hitting chapters in all of Jesus' experience. Study the whole chapter, and you will see that Jesus uses words such as "you hypocrites," you "blind guides," "you blind fools," and "you snakes," "you brood of vipers." Now how in the world can you say those words and have tears in your voice? I do not know.

Gravel in my throat as I bark such words? Sure. But tears? Not hardly. And yet that's what Jesus had. For He promised that if *anyone* opens the door, He will come in, and a friendship will flourish. What a beautiful invitation from the One who rebukes and chastens because He loves!

Here's the bottom line: Jesus loves bank robbers and Jesuits and drug traffickers and teachers and athletes and Muslims and even Pharisees. All of us are beloved sinners. All of us are cherished children. All of us are in need of God's grace.

Again, the Story

So here's our story one more time. To priests and rabbis and pastors and vegans and Sabbath keepers and Republicans who picket abortion clinics and rail on homosexuals, a wise Teacher told this story: "Two men went up to Notre Dame Cathedral to pray—one a committed Christian quarterback who was worshiped around the world for his good deeds, and the other a coach, a known pedophile. The quarterback stood by the altar and prayed: 'God, I thank You that You can use me to build churches and schools and hospitals and orphanages around the world. Thank You, God, for using me to star in a pro-life commercial during the Super Bowl. I thank You, O God, for the public platform upon which I pray and witness to millions. Thank You for the privilege of sharing Your love to the terminally ill before games. I gladly surrender my substantial tithe to Your cause. Grant me strength to fast and pray and serve You. Amen.'

"But the coach stood at a distance. He would not even look up to heaven, but succumbed to long, jagged sobs in a fetal position on the floor. 'Oh, my God. Oh, God, God,' he labored, 'have mercy on me. There is no human being less deserving and more despicable than me. For my appalling acts of cruelty to kids, I deserve to be tortured and crucified. God, have mercy on me.'

"I tell you the truth," said the wise Teacher, "this coach, rather than the quarterback, went home justified before God. For all those who exalt themselves will be humbled, and those who humble themselves will be exalted. Let those who have ears to hear, let them hear what the Spirit says. Amen."

The Classroom

First-Grade Art

Second-Grade Computers

Posting the paraphrase of Christ's parable (Luke 18:9–14) on Facebook sparked a lot of conversation. Here's a sampling of the comments:

- "Compelling message and challenge to . . . consider the condition of our respective souls; our desperate need for His amazing grace and abiding love!"
- "Makes me contemplate a lot!"
- "*Ooh,* this got me choked up!"
- "Golden nuggets of truth."
- "Very powerful parable to those of us 'inside' the church."

Third-Grade Bible

"If you walk around with your nose in the air, you're going to end up flat on your face, but if you're content to be simply yourself, you will become more than yourself" (Luke 18:14, *The Message*).

"If you're a know-it-all professor who thinks you've got God all figured out and you lord it over the lowly fifth-graders, watch out! You could wind up in kindergarten. But if you admit you ain't perfect, well, then God can use you" (Luke 18:14, our paraphrase).

Fourth-Grade Writing

I've heard Dad preach this chapter. He really likes the sermon. I told him, "Dad, you're a little too proud of this sermon on humility. Remember: 'Those who exalt themselves will be humbled, and those who humble themselves will be exalted' " (Luke 18:14, NLT).

Here's my takeaway from the chapter: Don't be full of yourself. Accept yourself as a sinner. Don't pretend you're not, because we all are.

Fifth-Grade Math

(Good Works)$^\infty$ = Mountain of Garbage
Here's another math equation of the chapter:

$$Pious\ Praying + (Fasting \times 100) + \left(\frac{Tithing}{100\%} \right) < Authenticity + Humility$$

Endnotes

1. Rick Reilly, "I Believe in Tim Tebow," ESPN, accessed August 18, 2013 http://espn.go.com/espn/story/_/id/7455943/believing-tim-tebow.

2. Jon Acuff, "How to Welcome People to Your Church," Jon Acuff, accessed March 4, 2013, http://www.jonacuff.com/stuffchristianslike/2012/07/how-to-welcome-people-to-your-church/. Web site is no longer active.

3. Jerry Bridges, *Holiness Day by Day: Transformational Thoughts for Your Spiritual Journey* (Colorado Springs, CO: NavPress, 2008), Kindle edition.

- 4 -

STEPS TO CHRIST

I was in New York City riding an elevator up to the top floor of the Empire State Building. As I reached the sixty-sixth floor, who should walk in but Donald Trump! I didn't expect to see him there. I figured he was off golfing at one of his famed resorts, but there was no mistaking that homely comb-over. It was definitely "The Donald."

I didn't want him to know that I recognized him, but I kept peeking at him out of the corner of my eye. Together we were ascending to the top floor. Pretty soon, he noticed me staring. He asked me, "Do you know who I am?"

"I'm not sure," I replied, "but you're sure handsome."

I wanted to buy a Jaguar. So I figured I'd treat him nice. We got to the top floor, and I made sure he got out of the elevator first. We went over to the edge, and we stared at the stirring streets of New York City far below. As we looked, he turned to me and said, "I have a proposition I'd like to make you."

"Is that so? What is it?" I was hanging on his every word.

"I'd like to give you a million dollars, on two conditions. Number one: you've got to promise me to spend the whole million dollars in one year."

Now, if I were going to get a million dollars, I would prefer to spread the fun out over a longer period of time. But if that was one of the conditions, I was willing. So I said, "OK, sir."

He continued, "The second condition is that wherever you are at the end of the year, you come back and meet me here. And there's no way of getting out of it. You meet me here at this same spot. If you don't, I have some men who will bring you here. And then you have to jump off and splat on the cement below."

I thought for a minute about that proposition. I looked at Mr. Trump and said, "Donald, you're ugly." I turned around, went back into the elevator, and descended to the street below, thinking how stupid a person would be to make that deal. Who would ever take him up on it?

That was a parable.

My father came to me one time when I was a boy with the same proposition in his imagination. He followed it with this: "Suppose that I am the enemy of every person in this world, and I come to you and say I have a proposition to make. You can do anything you want—no rules or regulations. Live it up for seventy years. That's the first condition. You have to put it all into seventy years. And the second condition is that at the end of seventy years, you come and go into the lake of fire with me."

Dad asked me, "Are you aware that a lot of folk take the devil up on that deal?"

"Yes."

I wonder which would be more stupid, to take seventy years and toss away eternity, or to take one year and chuck the seventy? If I think it would be stupid to take one year (even if I had a million dollars) when I had seventy to live, then wouldn't it be even crazier to take seventy years at the cost of eternity?

It would be eternally stupid. And so with a little common sense, I say, "Yes, I'm interested. I'm interested in this plan of salvation; I want eternal life." Perhaps it starts with a purely selfish motivation—a heaven to win and a hell to shun. And by the way, if God cannot reach me any other way, He will reach me right there. Are you aware of that?

If my motives are rotten, only God can transform my motives. I can't. So I'm interested in eternal life. My primary focus is not the Lord Jesus; it is to get in on heaven. And gradually, I begin to take those steps that every person takes in coming to Christ.

What are these steps? If you carefully study the book *Steps to Christ* and compare it with the Bible's instruction concerning salvation, you'll discover that the steps we take in coming to Christ are as follows, and in this order.

1. Desire

Our journey to Jesus always begins with a desire for something better. We may not be aware of this desire. It may not feel like a spiritual quest. We just know, down deep, that there's got to be something better than what we are experiencing in the present. And so we search.

Alcohol, fame, money, sex, power, promotions—these and a fat atlas of other dead ends are the avenues we pursue in our quest to address a deep, disquieting desire. Ultimately, only God can fill this chasm of emptiness. Everybody in the world is looking for God, but most seekers don't know it. From the executive in the penthouse office to the drunk in the gutter, the human heart is looking for something better.

Many years ago, my phone rang at 3:00 a.m. "Um, ah, hello?" I fumbled for a light switch.

"Pastor Haffner?"

"Yes?"

"Officer Jeb Reynolds here with the Bellevue Police. We have a young man in custody who claims he is in your youth group. Do you suppose you could come and pick him up?"

"Sure, I'll be right over." It wasn't until I was halfway there that it dawned on me that I had no clue who might be in trouble. Upon my arrival, the policeman ushered me into the security holding area near the back of the station. My heart quickened when the door locked behind me. Entering a plain concrete block, I obeyed the officer's gesture and sat in a wooden chair next to Ben.*

"Hi, Pastor Karl." Ben stared at his black work boots. "Thanks for coming. Last time this happened my mom said she ain't gonna come get me here again. So, thanks."

"Want to talk about what happened?" I asked.

Ben picked at a scab on his tattooed forearm. He fidgeted for a while, constantly twirling his greasy hair. "Ah, well, I dunno," he mumbled.

Then the strangest thing happened. Ben cried.

Being the consummate tough guy, always scoffing from the sidelines of our youth group, I never imagined Ben being so vulnerable. Tears splashed on his black leather jacket. Regaining his composure, he opened up. "I was at a party," he said. "I remember downing a few beers, and there was some pot there. I might have done some other drugs; I really don't remember. Anyway, the next thing I knew, I woke up here. You were the only guy that I could think of to call. I hope you don't mind."

"Not at all. I'm glad you did."

There was a long pause. His bloodshot eyes moistened again. "Oh, Pastor Karl, I hate myself. I'm wrecking my life. I'm sixteen, and I'm nothing but a strung-out, drugged-up alcoholic. I feel so empty. I hate myself, and I hate my life, but I feel helpless to change. That U2 song is the theme of my life—'I still haven't found what I'm looking for.' "

Last I heard, Ben's still searching. Now, however, his detours to jail last longer, and nobody comes to pick him up. He keeps trying to fill a God-shaped vacuum with drugs and booze and parties, but he's still coming up empty. In that respect, Ben is like most every person I know.

Whether it's eating, shopping, doing drugs, or taking care of others, we're addicts, aren't we? An addiction, after all, is anything we use to fill the empty place inside of us that belongs to God alone. Until God plugs that hole, we'll forever be singing that old tune, "I still haven't found what I'm looking for."

2. UNDERSTANDING

The second step in coming to Jesus requires an understanding of the character of God and the plan of salvation. According to Morrie Venden, this knowledge must grasp the love, kindness, and mercy of God. After all, Venden argues, it is possible to have just head knowledge of Scripture. The people in Christ's day searched the Scriptures plenty. And yet Jesus said to them, "You study the Scriptures diligently because you think that in them you have eternal life. These are the

---

* Not his real name.

very Scriptures that testify about me, yet you refuse to come to me to have life" (John 5:39, 40). It is possible to use Scripture as a convenient escape from seeking Jesus. A person can analyze, dissect, and approach Scripture as pure theory and miss out on salvation.

The devil knows that this is an essential step, so he'll do everything in his power to steer the seeker off course and on to a detour. Realize that all of his methods boil down to one common denominator: to get people to misunderstand God. He wants us to see God as a cruel tyrant. He paints God as a vengeful, angry dictator hell-bent on destroying the human race. The devil wants you to blame God for the tornadoes, tsunamis, divorces, riots, and rapes.

Thus, it is critical to have a truthful picture of God. How you understand God determines what you will do with God and His offer of salvation. It all boils down to your picture of Him.

Take, for example, the stark juxtaposition of the prayers of the passengers on United Airlines Flight 93 with those of the terrorists. This was the flight hijacked by four al-Qaeda terrorists on September 11, 2001. It crashed into a field in Pennsylvania during an attempt by some of the passengers to regain control of the plane, killing all forty-four people aboard including the four hijackers.

The movie *United 93* portrays how several passengers were able to make telephone calls and learn that attacks had already been carried out by other hijacked airliners on the World Trade Center in New York City and the Pentagon outside Washington, D.C. Some of the passengers then attempt to regain control of the aircraft. Just before the climactic scene when Todd Beamer gives his now-famous command, "Let's roll," he pauses with his colleagues, and they pray that God will help them in their mission. Ironically, the terrorists know of the impending counterattack, so they, too, pray that God will make them successful in their mission.

So which mission should God bless? Whose prayer gets answered? How is it that both the terrorists and the passengers can solicit the help of God when their missions are so starkly opposed to each other? Clearly, the two groups embrace radically different pictures of God.

To have an accurate picture of God is a crucial step in understanding and experiencing salvation. John 14 says it very clearly: Jesus is what God has always been like; Jesus is what God is like today; and Jesus is what God will always be like.

The devil knows that you need to have a friendly God in order for people to be interested in becoming acquainted with Him. And he knows that becoming acquainted with God is the whole shebang. And so he is constantly trying to produce an unfriendly God.

A student once told me, "I kinda like Jesus, but I don't like God." This represents a misunderstanding that is held by many people. Truth is, Jesus and God are the same. So if you come to know and love and trust Jesus, you will also know and love and trust God. You will realize, then, that God is Someone who really is out for your best good. As Pastor Dwight Nelson is known to say, "God is not someone to be afraid of. He is someone to be a friend of." The devil hates that idea. But this realization will lead us to the third step.

3. CONVICTION

Understanding God's love and His good character then convicts the sinner of the need for forgiveness of sin. But what is sin all about? Typically, we think of sin in terms of doing bad things. But the apostle John says that the Holy Spirit is going to reprove the world of sin because they believe not on Jesus, that is, they don't trust Jesus. "When he [the Holy Spirit] comes, he will prove the world to be in the wrong about sin and righteousness and judgment: about sin, because people do not believe in me" (John 16:8, 9).

With sin, the primary issue is not trusting Jesus, not believing Him. Don't buy into the misunderstanding that sin is bad behavior; at the heart of sin is a broken relationship.

Morrie Venden suggests that Eve sinned *before* she ate the apple. Eating the apple was the *result* of her sin. First, she distrusted God. She embraced a convoluted notion about His character. And you know the rest of the story.

Eve was walking in the Garden. She came near the tree. The serpent was in the tree. He looked out through the leaves of the tree and said, "Hi, Eve." Eve was startled; she looked into the tree.

The serpent said, "You're surprised that I know how to talk, aren't you?"

Eve said, "As a matter of fact, the thought had crossed my mind."

The serpent came through with his big one: "If I, a dumb creature, can eat of the fruit and learn to talk, what do you suppose would happen to you, someone who already knows how to talk, if you ate the fruit? Why, you would become as God."

Eve swallowed it.

She distrusted God. She believed the serpent. She was no longer under the conviction that God was really looking out for her best good, and, at that point, she sinned. As a result of her sin, she ate the apple.

When we come under the conviction that we are sinners, it is a far different thing than coming under the conviction that we have sinned. The Ten Commandments convict us that we have sinned—that is, that we have done bad things. Looking at God, as revealed in Jesus Christ, convicts us that we are sinners. Whether or not we have ever done any bad things is not the issue. We are born into the world of sin; we are born with sinful natures.

You may object: "Cute, innocent babies are—born sinners? Really? Born with a desire to kill and steal and lie and cheat?"

No, but the innocent little baby was born with one thing in common with all babies born into this world—every baby is born self-centered. And it is because of this selfish nature, which carries with it all of the roots of lying and stealing and cheating and killing, that the only way for that child to be saved in God's kingdom is to be born again. In other words, there is something wrong with our first birth. But the glorious truth is that God has never held us accountable for being born sinners. He has never held that against us. Aren't you glad for that? He understands the dilemma in which we were born. He's very patient with us. The only thing that God holds us responsible for is what we do with the Lord Jesus Christ who came to save sinners. And that's good news.

Let's be clear now on the difference between sin and sins. *Sin,* singular, is living a life independently of Jesus Christ. We were born, selfish in nature, into sin. *Sins,* plural, are the transgressions of God's law. Sins are the bad behaviors that flow out of a nature of sin.

So if you and I are having a problem with sin, should we work harder on our sins? What's our real problem? Where do we put our efforts? If sins are the result of sin, where do we put our effort—toward the problem or toward the symptoms? Ever try putting a bandage on cancer? It won't work. Ever try fixing your sins? It won't work.

Because of our birth, we find it natural to do wrong. And as long as we continue to live lives apart from Jesus Christ, it is natural for us to do wrong. So when the Holy Spirit convicts us that we are sinners, it is only natural for us to start working on our bad behaviors. The devil laughs. The strong person with lots of willpower, the stubborn Dutchman from South Dakota, tricks himself into thinking that he succeeds in working on his sins because he can prevail outwardly. But inside, he's still the same. The strong person fools herself into thinking she is a success outwardly and becomes proud of her external goodness, but her image management counts for nothing.

The weak person works on the sins and fails time and again. Discouragement follows, and so often the struggling Christian gives up altogether on God.

Whether you are strong willed or weak willed, working on your sins is always a dead-end street. Being convicted that our DNA is sin and that we will never find deliverance from our sins or sin apart from Jesus, sets us on the pathway to salvation. It leads us to the fourth step.

4. Helplessness

The Bible teaches that we are utterly helpless when it comes to being good in our own strength.

Jeremiah wonders, "Can an Ethiopian change his skin or a leopard its spots? Neither can you do good who are accustomed to doing evil" (Jeremiah 13:23).

Jesus teaches, "I am the vine; you are the branches. If you remain in me and I in you, you will bear much fruit; apart from me you can do nothing" (John 15:5).

Apart from Jesus, we are helpless to do anything at all about our spiritual condition. Admitting our helplessness is to focus on God's power, not willpower. Try all you like, but you will always be helpless to muster up enough willpower to change the color of your skin or to overcome your sin (singular, meaning your sinful nature).

A popular children's story called *Frog and Toad Together* touches on the futility of willpower. In the story, Frog bakes a batch of cookies.

"We ought to stop eating," Frog and Toad say, as they keep consuming cookies.

"We must stop," they resolve, as they eat more. "We need willpower," Frog emphatically declares.

"What is willpower?" asks Toad, swallowing another mouthful.

"Willpower is trying very hard not to do something you want to do very much," Frog says.

Then Frog suggests boosting their willpower by putting the cookies high in a tree, but Toad points out, between bites, that they could still climb the tree and get them. In desperation, Frog dumps the cookies on the ground. "Hey, birds!" he calls. "Here are the cookies!"

"Now we have no more cookies," says Toad sadly.

"Yes," says Frog, "but we have lots and lots of willpower."

"You can keep it all," Toad replies. "I'm going home to bake a cake."[1]

In seeking a deep life with God, willpower is not the answer. You can try really hard to stop sinning, but it's only a matter of time until you're back to the case of cookies. You see, the experience of salvation is not about trying really hard to be good. It's all about living in the presence of our God who is good. As you admit your helplessness and live in His presence, you are then changed into His likeness, and the cookies no longer hold the same power that they once did. But make no mistake; the power is God's power, not willpower. You are helpless to save yourself. And you are helpless to change yourself.

To say we are helpless is not to suggest that we are worthless. Please note the difference between helplessness and worthlessness.

We are worth the entire universe in the sight of God. The Cross testifies that we are worth everything. But we're still helpless to change our lives apart from Jesus. And when we give up, only then can we come to Christ. How? We come on our knees before His open Word—that's the way it's done. And we come with a sense of helplessness, having given up on ourselves. We pray, "God, there's not a chance in the world that I can meet You in Your kingdom. There's not a chance in the world that I can be the kind of Christian I want to be. If anything gets done about my life, You're going to have to do it. I can't." The painful truth is that no one ever comes to Christ until they've reached that point.

"The Lord can do nothing toward the recovery of man until, convinced of his own weakness and stripped of all self-sufficiency, he yields himself to the control of God. Then he can receive the gift that God is waiting to bestow."[2]

5. SURRENDER

The fifth and final step, then, is to give up. In a word, it is to surrender.

Surrender, if we understand it correctly, is not—as we often think—the surrender of our sins. It is not primarily saying, "From now on, I'm *not* going to smoke or drink or dance or listen to raunchy rap music or read trashy novels."

Surrender is the surrender of self. Surrender is admitting that we can't do anything about our smoking, drinking, dancing, chewing, and carousing. Surrender is admitting that there's not a thing we can do that counts toward salvation. It means responding to Jesus who knocks at the door and inviting Him to live in us and change us from within.

A friend of mine slaved one summer on a garbage crew. The long, muggy days got more than a bit monotonous. To break the boredom, one morning the crew decorated their truck. Wrapping it in streamers and posters, they advertised, "Just married." Passersby honked and laughed and waved. Clearly, however, they were still driving a garbage truck.

Likewise, many Christians try to decorate the externals with trimmings of godliness. They obsess with cosmetic Christianity and external measures of righteousness. Unless there is a full-on, complete surrender, however, it's like decorating a garbage truck. Try all you want to wear the right posters and streamers in order to craft what other people see, your true nature will always betray you. Sorry trashbreath, but you won't fool anybody—especially God.

That's why the apostle Paul adamantly spoke of surrendering one's sinful nature "with its passions and desires" (Galatians 5:24). To the Christians in Rome, he wrote, "Or don't you know that all of us who were baptized into Christ Jesus were baptized into his death? We were therefore buried with him through baptism into death in order that, just as Christ was raised from the dead through the glory of the Father, we too may live a new life" (Romans 6:3, 4).

When Paul refers to baptism, he is talking about more than the cosmetics. He's not suggesting cute placards to garnish the outside of a truck. He's talking about getting a new vehicle, which means surrendering everything. In Bible times, Paul's audience understood that baptism signified a complete transformation. It was not a covering up of sin; it was a radical change in the nature of the sinner.

Once at a baptism, I lowered a young woman into the water but failed to completely submerge her. Oh, she was almost drenched, but a section on her bangs remained dry. Nobody would have known, except me. Perhaps I'm all wet on this one, but I couldn't stomach the thought of an incomplete baptism. To me, that feels like an incomplete surrender. What an oxymoron! So I scooped up a handful of water and splashed it on her forehead while disguising it in a hug! I exhaled a big *"Ahhhhh!"* For the record, my hang-up is biblical. Baptism symbolizes a total transformation, that is, a completely new life.

Only when this new life takes root does one experience the character change that seeps through every arena of being. Television viewing, video games, Web sites visited—all of these things that command our time will be altered by our conversion to Christ. In a sense, when Christ occupies first place, we hand over the remote control and let Him determine the programming. This is how He changes us from the inside out. And it's the only kind of change that interests God.

If anyone tries to tell you differently, trust me—they're full of garbage.

THE CLASSROOM

FIRST-GRADE ART

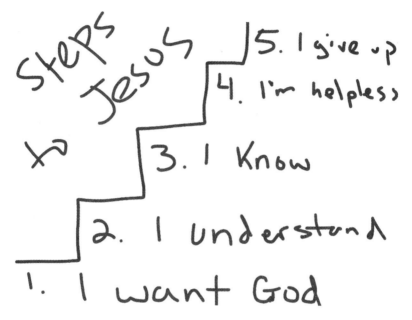

Steps to Jesus

5. I give up
4. I'm helpless
3. I Know
2. I understand
1. I want God

SECOND-GRADE COMPUTERS

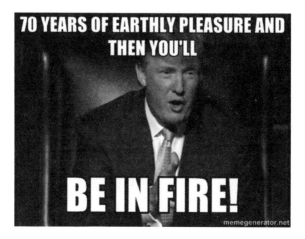

70 YEARS OF EARTHLY PLEASURE AND THEN YOU'LL BE IN FIRE!

memegenerator.net

THIRD-GRADE BIBLE

"When the Helper comes, he will prove to the people of the world the truth about sin, about being right with God, and about judgment. He will prove to them that sin is not believing in me. He will prove to them that being right with God comes from my going to the Father and not being seen anymore" (John 16:8–10, NCV).

God versus the people of the world

"Heretofore unseen, a Holy Witness will one day come with duly sworn allegiance to and from the Holy Judge and will render proof of the errancy of the world's view on sin, righteousness, and judgment. The Holy Witness will testify to and prove the existence of their transgression of the law solely as the rejection of Christ, presenting irrefutable evidence that legal innocence before the Holy Judge is based only on the advocacy efforts of our Defense Attorney" (John 16:8–10, our paraphrase).

Fourth-Grade Writing

Charles Haddon Spurgeon said, "Do you think to come to Jesus up the ladder of knowledge? Come down, sir; you will meet him at the foot."

Fifth-Grade Math

Desire + Understanding + Conviction + Helplessness + Surrender = Jesus

Endnotes

1. Arnold Lobel, *Frog and Toad Together* (Columbus, OH: Newfield Publications, 1972), 30–41.

2. Ellen White, *The Desire of Ages* (Mountain View, CA: Pacific Press® Publishing Association, 1940), 300.

− 5 −

KNOWING FOR SURE

Several years ago, I was in love with this beautiful girl, and we decided to be married. I was living down near Los Angeles; she was living up near San Francisco. Her parents put on the wedding, like parents are supposed to do. I traveled north for the wedding and stood before our families, friends, and the preacher.

The preacher asked, "Wilt thou?" and we wilted, and that was that. We were married.

After the wedding, she went home to her folks, and I went back to Los Angeles.

Two years later, someone said to me one day, "Are you married?"

"Yes."

He said, "Where's your wife?"

"Well, the last I saw her she was in San Francisco."

He asked, "When was that?"

I said, "Two years ago."

"And you've had no contact with her? Do you write?"

"No."

"E-mail?"

"No."

"Text?"

"No."

"Facebook?"

"No."

"Instant message?"

"No."

"Call?"

"No."

"Haven't you seen her since?"

"No."

"And you're married?"

"Yes. I said, 'I do.' I said, 'Yes' two years ago."

He said, "You better go check."

That was a parable.

A marriage is based upon a relationship, and a relationship is based on communication. There is no such thing as a continuing marriage unless there is a continuing of the marriage. We don't believe in once married, always married unless you keep married.

Neither do we believe once saved, always saved unless you keep saved.

Sarah Hinlicky Wilson pictures a bride and a groom dashing out of the chapel into a waiting limo. Imagine if the first thing the groom said to his wife was this:

> "Now you realize, my dear," he begins, "that, as far as I'm concerned, we can't really say we're married, because I don't know yet what kind of wife you'll turn out to be. I hope for the best, of course. And I'll help you all I can. But only at the end of our lives will I be able to tell if you've lived up to my expectations. If you have—then, and only then, I'll agree that we truly got married today. But if you don't, then as far as I'm concerned we were never married at all."[1]

No! The couple that has been married for five minutes is just as married as the couple celebrating fifty-five years of marriage. Likewise, the Christian who accepted Jesus Christ five minutes ago is just as saved as the person who accepted Jesus fifty-five years ago. Your ensuing good deeds or bad deeds do not compromise your "married-ness." The marital relationship tops your matrimonial rifts.

SECURELY CONNECTED

So is it possible to feel the same security in your relationship with Jesus? Can your assurance of salvation supersede your doubts when you screw up? Can we know, for sure, that we are saved?

Take surveys of young or old people, and you will discover that the number one question about faith and spirituality is this: How can I be certain of my salvation?

Can I propose that this indicates that a lot of folk are uncertain of their salvation?

Why the doubt? Morrie Venden suggests that it is because we are constantly deciding whether or not we are saved or have the certainty of salvation on the basis of our behavior.

Listen up. Our behavior and our good deeds have nothing whatever to do with the reality of our salvation. Good works are very important; but our works, our obedience, our good deeds in living the Christian life have nothing to do whatsoever with securing our salvation.

Now take it a step further. Our bad deeds, therefore, have nothing to do with causing us to be lost. Ouch! I've tried out the first statement on ministers, and they say, "That's right, our good works do not cause our salvation." Then I throw the corollary out there, and they want to throw me out!

Here's the truth: we are saved or we are lost based totally on the presence or absence of a vital relationship with the Lord Jesus Christ. Now this in no way opens the door for license because a vital relationship with anybody is the greatest single safeguard against license.

The great experience of salvation through faith in Jesus Christ alone is the only thing that produces good works, but good works have nothing to do with causing our salvation. We do not change our lives in order to come to Christ. We come to Christ just as we are, and He changes our lives.

Ellen White puts it this way:

> The power of Christ alone can work the transformation in heart and mind that all must experience who would partake with Him of the new life in the kingdom of heaven. "Except a man be born again," the Saviour has said, "he cannot see the kingdom of God." John 3:3. The religion that comes from God is the only religion that can lead to God. In order to serve Him aright, we must be born of the divine Spirit. This will lead to watchfulness. It will purify the heart and renew the mind, and give us a new capacity for knowing and loving God. It will give us willing obedience to all His requirements.[2]

Now, if I'm supposed to receive a "willing obedience" to *all* of God's requirements at the point of conversion, then I'm dead. I begin to wonder if I was ever converted. Have you ever experienced something of the power of God, but discovered later that you still had seeds of resistance in you, that you're still falling and failing?

Do you remember twelve disciples who walked along the dusty roads with Jesus, who were bickering and arguing about who was going to be the greatest? Did they realize what they were doing? Well, they kept lagging farther and farther behind Jesus, perhaps so they could fight louder and louder. When they finally arrived at the next town, they were a half-mile behind Jesus!

They knew what they were doing. They had been behaving this way for three years, and now one of the last things they did just before the Crucifixion was to bicker and argue in the upper room about who was going to be the greatest. So when it came to having a "willing obedience to all of [Christ's] requirements," they had problems.

When they arrived, Jesus asked them, "So what were you gents talking about?"

"Well, um, ah, nice day in Galilee, isn't it?"

BORN AGAIN

Again, Ellen White's insights are helpful. She writes, "The Saviour said, 'Except a man be born from above,' unless he shall receive a new heart, new desires, purposes, and motives, *leading to a new life,* 'he cannot see the kingdom of God.' "[3] When we are born again, we receive new hearts that *lead* to new lives. If that doesn't happen, then spiritually speaking, we're dead.

The next time you feel the miraculous power of God in your life, but then you botch things up again and you think, *Well, now I've messed up again, so I guess it wasn't real. I'm still falling. I'm still failing. I still have struggles with my weaknesses,* recognize the voice of the snake, and don't let the enemy clobber you again.

Accept the fact that God is at work and He *will* lead you to a new life. "We shall often have to bow down and weep at the feet of Jesus because of our short-comings and mistakes," says Ellen White, "but we are not to be discouraged. Even if we are overcome by the enemy, we are not cast off, not forsaken and rejected of God."[4] "Christ Jesus who died—more than that, who was raised to life—is at the right hand of God and is also interceding for us" (Romans 8:34).

John, the same disciple who aspired to become the greatest in the kingdom, would later write this: "My dear children, I write this to you so that you will not sin. But if anybody does sin, we have an advocate with the Father—Jesus Christ, the Righteous One" (1 John 2:1).

God knows that in the struggling Christian life, we are going to fall and fail and flop, but that's where the growth takes place. So the next time you fail in your Christian life, don't sit around for two weeks waiting for God to cool off before you come back. The fact is, in the Christian life, we will often need to "bow down and weep at the feet of Jesus because of our shortcomings and mistakes, but we are not to be discouraged." We are not cast off by God. These concepts, in themselves, prove that the certainty of our salvation is based on something different than our good deeds or misdeeds. John 17:3 states it so clearly: "Now this is eternal life: that they know you, the only true God, and Jesus Christ, whom you have sent."

There are only two kinds of people in the world: those who know God, and those who don't. And both kinds are in every church, including your own. All Christians are not Seventh-day Adventists, and all Seventh-day Adventists are not Christians. A Christian is one who has a personal acquaintance with the Lord Jesus Christ.

In the book *Steps to Christ,* it says that a selfish heart can perform generous actions. Let's say I'm a shoe cobbler and I move to Berrien Springs, Michigan. I want to open up a business. When I discover that much of the town is comprised of church people, it would only make sense for me to join the Adventist Church in order to have a thriving business, right? Perhaps I should try to be a deacon.

"Who is that passing the offering?"

"Oh, that's the new shoe cobbler."

"Oh yeah, I'd better go get my shoes fixed."

We can have all kinds of wrong reasons for doing the right things. So how are we going to know whether we are really followers of Christ? Ellen White answers,

A selfish heart may perform generous actions. By what means, then, shall we determine whose side we are on?

Who has the heart? With whom are our thoughts? Of whom do we love to converse? Who has our warmest affections and our best energies? If we are Christ's, our thoughts are with Him, and our sweetest thoughts are of Him. All we have and are is consecrated to Him. We long to bear His image, breathe His spirit, do His will, and please Him in all things.[5]

Do you find yourself spontaneously thinking of Jesus, something from His life, as you go about the campus? Do you find yourself thinking about something from the life of Jesus while driving down the highway or doing the dishes? When you are eating lunch? The only way that this happens is by constant fellowship and communication with Jesus.

The certainty of your salvation is based not only upon the fact that you experienced the regenerating power of the Holy Spirit two years ago or twenty-two years ago; the certainty of your salvation continues to be based upon your continuing relationship with Jesus.

This doesn't add anything to Christ's finished work—absolutely not, any more than my continued communication with my wife will add anything to the "I do" and the legal document that is in the courthouse. But if I do not know what it means to have faith and trust in God and maintain a vital day by day connection with Him, then I am no longer righteous. And "the LORD knoweth the way of the righteous: but the way of the ungodly shall perish" (Psalm 1:6, KJV). Salvation is based upon Jesus Christ alone, but its application in my life has to be by an initial acceptance of Him plus a continuing fellowship with Him.

In the experience of the Christian, the devotional life is not optional. Many people have the idea that it is a nice thing to do. Why, you know, if you have some time, read the Bible, pray; it will make God feel good. And there are some people we feel are kind of geared that way, you know, the mystics. They are the ones who can sense the presence of God and practice the presence of God, right? But me? No way. So I'll try something else.

Let's be clear: *there is nothing else to try!*

If, as a Christian, you haven't yet discovered meaning in the personal, daily devotional life and a friendship with Jesus, don't try anything else. I repeat, *There is nothing else to try!* There is nothing else. And it is not optional any more than communication with my wife is optional in a good marriage. This is the entire basis of the Christian experience. It all boils down to an ongoing communion and fellowship with Jesus.

Jesus longs to spend time with you. Have you allowed space for Him to join you during this day? He wants to abide in your home.

Have you invited Him in?

And when He comes in, on a day-by-day basis, He will bring you peace—one of the trademarks of an authentic Christian life. "Submit to God and be at peace with him" (Job 22:21). "Since we have been justified through faith, we have peace with God through our Lord Jesus Christ" (Romans 5:1).

The only thing that we can do to become and remain Christians is to know this fellowship, this relationship with Jesus. That's all.

That's all!

BLESSED ASSURANCE

The author of Hebrews states clearly that we can enjoy the "full assurance" of salvation. How? All we must do is to "draw near to God with a sincere heart" (Hebrews 10:22). Stay close to God in friendship with Him, and you will be cleansed "from a guilty conscience . . . washed with pure water" (verse 22). You can know for sure that your salvation is secure as long as you know Him!

One author puts it this way: "The Scriptures teach that we can know with absolute certainty that we have the life of God within us (1 John 4:13). This confidence is not based on inner feelings or outward signs. Rather, this 'blessed assurance' is founded upon the promises of a faithful God and this inspired Word."[6] Assurance is not based on the amount of our faith but upon the object of our faith—Jesus Christ!

Fanny Crosby captured this truth in her timeless hymn "Blessed Assurance." Though blinded at six weeks of age through improper medical treatment, Crosby wrote more than eight thousand hymns in her lifetime of ninety-five years.

As the story goes, one day Phoebe Knapp, a friend and the daughter of a noted Methodist evangelist, visited Fanny in her New York home. "Oh, Fanny," she said, "I have had a new melody racing through my mind for some time now, and I just can't think of anything else. Let me play it for you, and perhaps you can help me with the words."

"After kneeling in prayer and clutching her little Bible, the blind poetess stood to her feet with face aglow: 'Why, that music says, "Blessed Assurance, Jesus is mine! O what a foretaste of glory divine." ' "[7]

Expressed in that song is the simple truth that salvation is sure, so long as we continue to nurture a friendship with Jesus. "This is my story, this is my song, praising my Savior all the day long!"

THE CLASSROOM

FIRST-GRADE ART

Worried about your salvation? Take to heart the words of Jesus: "Look at the birds in the sky. They do not plant seeds. They do not gather grain. They do not put grain into a building to keep. Yet your Father in heaven feeds them! Are you not more important than the birds? Which of you can make himself a little taller by worrying? Why should you worry about clothes? Think how the flowers grow. They do not work or make cloth. But I tell you that Solomon in all his greatness was not dressed as well as one of these flowers. God clothes the grass of the field. It lives today and is burned in the stove tomorrow. How much more will He give you clothes? You have so little faith! Do not worry. Do not keep saying, 'What will we eat?' or, 'What will we drink?' or, 'What will we wear?' The people who do not know God are looking for all these things. Your Father in heaven knows you need all these things. First of all, look for the holy nation of God. Be right with Him. All these other things will be given to you also. Do not worry about tomorrow. Tomorrow will have its own worries. The troubles we have in a day are enough for one day" (Matthew 6:26–34, NLV).

Second-Grade Computers

 If you're into social media at all, then you probably belong to the LinkedIn network of 225 million people who participate in this online community of professionals. Go to its homepage, and you'll see LinkedIn's threefold mission, which captures the core of Christian assurance:

1. **"Connect. Find/Be found."** It all starts by connecting with Christ, right? Search for Jesus, and you will find Him. Moreover, you will be found!
2. **"Power your career."** All power in the Christian's life comes from Christ—power to save, power to change, power to experience security in Him.
3. **"Learn and share."** Salvation is a journey in Jesus. Through a growing relationship with Him, we learn. We share Him. And we can know that our salvation is sure.

Third-Grade Bible

"And this is the way to have eternal life—to know you, the only true God, and Jesus Christ, the one you sent to earth" (John 17:3, NLT).

"The only way to know you are saved is to know Jesus Christ" (John 17:3, our paraphrase).

Fourth-Grade Writing

Augustine said, "To be assured of our salvation is no arrogant stoutness. It is faith. It is devotion. It is not presumption. It is God's promise."

Fifth-Grade Math

No Jesus = No Salvation
Know Jesus = Know Salvation

Endnotes

1. Sarah Hinlicky Wilson, "What's His Is Ours," *Christianity Today,* September 2012, 32.

2. Ellen G. White, *Testimonies for the Church* (Mountain View, CA: Pacific Press®, 1948), 9:156.

3. Ellen G. White, *Steps to Christ* (Washington, DC: Review and Herald®, 1956), 18; emphasis added.

4. White, *Steps to Christ,* 64.

5. Ibid., 58.

6. "The Story of Blessed Assurance," Bible Study Planet, accessed August 22, 2013, http://biblestudyplanet.com/the-story-of-blessed-assurance/.

7. Ibid.

- 6 -

STEPS IN CHRIST

Morris Venden loved to tell the following parable written by Bill Gravestock. I contacted Bill, who graciously gave me permission to reprint his classic story.

His story begins and ends in Mercy Hospital—in the intensive-care ward. The patient's name is Ben Trying. He'd been trying to be a Christian. He'd been trying to be good. He'd been trying to believe, to have faith, to break through—but it seemed useless, hopeless. And now he lay flat on his back with but a few brief hours to live. To him, time was very precious. He knew that he was breathing on borrowed time. He had no one to help him prepare for eternity except his three religious sisters. Each was a professed Christian. Each had come to comfort and console their dear brother in this tragic moment of crisis and grief. Maybe they could help him break through and believe before it was too late. Even now, they waited in the lobby of the intensive-care ward to see their dying brother.

The nurse whispered to one of the sisters, Miss Nebulous N. Tangible. She quietly followed the nurse and was told that she had three minutes. As she sat by the bedside of her dear, despairing brother and looked into his eyes, she knew that he was without God and without hope. He clutched her hand and moaned, "Please, sis, help me to break through . . . I don't . . . have much time. Help me to believe. Please help me."

How could he be helped? What could she say? She took a deep breath and began to speak.

"Ben, Ben, listen to me. You must give your heart to Jesus, quickly." Ben stared at her in disbelief. He moved his hand over his heart and looked puzzled. "You must reach out your hand and take His, then invite Him into your heart. You must behold the Lamb and turn away from sin and surrender all." Ben's expression conveyed confusion, so she continued. "You must fall on the Rock. You must rely on His merits and repent of your sins, then accept freely of His unconquerable robe of righteousness. This is your covering—your wedding garment. It is yours, Ben, when you repent and believe."

Beads of sweat rolled off his tired, worn face. His head lay back on the pillow as he stared hopelessly at the ceiling. A mournful sigh escaped his lips as he trembled

3—A.Y.M.S.T.F.G.

in despair. The nurse came in and whispered, "Miss Nebulous, your time is up."

The second sister, Miss Solid Ann Concrete, made her way into her brother's room and sat at his bedside. Before she could say anything, Ben looked frantically at her and with great effort forced out these words: "Oh, sis, please help me. Help me to believe. I'm trying . . . to break through, . . . but I can't . . . can't." She leaned over and looked into his face. It portrayed the anxiousness of his heart. She then took his trembling hand and said, "Ben, I can only tell you what the Bible says about the kind of people that will go to heaven. Their behavior will be in distinct contrast to that of the world. If you want to be there . . . well, it's up to you. But in order for you to have hope and in order for you to be a Christian, you must first renounce your old life of sin—your life of wickedness and selfishness. Your social habits—your behavior and conversation—must be drastically changed. Everything you do has got to go. It's evil. It's no good. I have to tell you the truth. You must give up your gambling. Stop smoking. Stop drinking. Quit going to those terrible bars and nightclubs. Change your habits. Don't associate with your old friends. Make new ones. Lose all that weight. Quit being a glutton. Make your body a fit place for the Lord to dwell. Allow only good and uplifting and ennobling thoughts to enter your mind. Stop reading those vile magazines and dirty stories. Instead, read the Bible. Fill your mind with things that are pure and lovely. Dwell on things in heaven. Love the Lord and hate evil with perfect hatred and . . . and . . . Ben! . . . Ben! . . . Are you listening? Ben? Are you all right? Nurse! Nurse!"

Ben gasped for breath. He choked and gagged. The nurse quickly took his pulse. "He's almost gone. Could you wait outside, please?"

Moments later, the nurse beckoned to the last sister. "Are you Ben's other sister?" she asked.

"Yes, I am."

"You don't have much time." The nurse paused, then added, "And neither does he."

"I understand, Nurse. Thank you so very much." Sitting beside her precious brother, Miss Faith N. Christ took his hand and prayed silently that her words would be a savor of life unto life to poor Ben, her wandering, lost baby brother. She looked into his eyes with hope and courage, and said, "Ben, are you ready to die?"

"No, I'm not ready, sis, but I'm trying to be ready. I'm . . . trying to break through. I'm trying to believe, . . . sis." He wrung his hands, and he wept as he sighed and shook his head. "But it's no use. I just can't believe. I just can't break through. I've tried as hard as I can, but it's no use . . . no use."

Faith leaned toward his ear as he lay there motionless. "My dear brother Ben, I understand your predicament. Would you just be still for a few minutes? Just be very quiet and listen. That's all I ask for you to do—just listen." As soon as he was calm, Faith began to speak. She did not urge him to try harder to believe;

instead, she gave him the assurance of how God the Father had loved him in Jesus Christ. She began to tell him the good news—the glad tidings. "Ben," she said, "while you were His enemy, the Father loved you and chose you to be with Him where He is. He spared not His only Son for you. All of heaven was emptied and went bankrupt for you. He's given all of the accumulated and hoarded love and wealth of eternity in the gift of Jesus, His Son. You have been redeemed, forgiven, and accepted in Jesus. Yes, God the Father has done all this for you by His grace, Ben. It is God's riches, at Christ's expense, by grace alone. The Father saves you by His grace.

"Two thousand years ago, when the fullness of the time had come, God the Son, your Savior Jesus, left heaven, because all of its stupendous glory was not a place to be desired while you were lost. He whom angels loved and worshiped stepped down from His exalted throne and position and condescended to come to this dark planet Earth. And at Heaven's appointed hour, He was born in a lowly stable for you, Ben. He grew up, lived, and suffered shame and humiliation as the rejected One in order that you might be the accepted one. For your sake, He became poor that through His poverty you might be rich. He was treated the way you deserve that you might be treated the way He deserves. He wore the crown of thorns that you might wear the crown of life. The vinegar and gall were His so that the honey and sweet might be yours. He paid the price that you might enjoy the inheritance. And by His crucifixion and death, He has taken your sins and put them in the tomb, burying the old life of failure forever. He's destroyed death, defeated the devil in your behalf, shut the gates of hell, and opened Paradise. We're saved by His work and not our own. He rose again the third day, and by the power of His resurrection and ascension, He's taken that perfect, flawless life and righteousness to the throne of God. The Father has received Him back— honored, embraced, and accepted as our Representative, as our Substitute in the place of our failure. And, Ben, when the Father received, honored, embraced, and accepted Jesus back, it was the same as if you were received, honored, embraced, and accepted, because your humanity was constituted in Him. Faith says, 'Mine are Christ's living, doing, and speaking, His suffering and dying; mine as much as if I had lived, done, spoken, and suffered, and died as He did.' All things necessary for your salvation have been done, Ben, through the doing and dying of Jesus. The warfare has been fought; the victory is accomplished. God the Son has reconciled you to the Father. By His death on the cross, you are pardoned. By His resurrection and life, you are promoted. It is by Christ alone. The Son saves you by His life and death.

"And that's not all, my precious brother. Even now, God the Holy Spirit is present to give you faith through the hearing of the gospel. It is His work to convict us of sin, righteousness, and judgment. It is His work to create faith in our hearts as the gospel is heard. He, too, loves you and will comfort you. He will illuminate your mind, show you the cross, draw you to Christ, and give you the blessed hope and joy of acceptance in loving fellowship with the Father and with the Son. He causes us to see the goodness of the Father in giving His Son, which leads us to repentance and gives us rich faith in His unspeakable love and mercy. Because only by love is love awakened.

"God the Father loves you and saves you by His grace in giving you His only Son. God the Son loves you and saves you by giving you His life, His death—His doing, His dying. God the Holy Spirit loves you and saves you by giving you faith to accept your acceptance and to believe on the name of the Son of God so that you may know, Ben, that you have eternal life, and this life is in His Son. He that has the Son has life."

Ben's ear had heard the everlasting gospel. Faith was kindled in his heart. He saw through the illumination of the Holy Spirit that he was accepted, because Jesus was acceptable. He saw that he was pleasing in God's sight, because Jesus was altogether pleasing. He grasped the simple truth that Jesus was his personal Representative and Substitute Righteousness at the Father's right hand. He realized now that the question was not, "Will God accept me?" but in the light of the gospel, the question is, "Will I accept the fact that I've been accepted?" He comprehended the amazing discovery that the very fact he was a sinner entitled him to come to Jesus.

There was no question now. There were no doubts. The Holy Spirit illuminated his mind, and little by little the chain of evidence was joined together. In Jesus—bruised, mocked, and hanging upon the cross—he saw the Lamb of God, which takes away the sin of the world. Hope flooded his soul. Now he knew and had the assurance and confidence and boldness that Jesus' life was his life. He knew now that his acceptance was sure, because he was accepted in the Beloved. Gratitude swelled in his heart for Jesus. Tears rolled down his cheeks. Joy filled his soul. A smile broke upon his face as he said, "I see it . . . I see . . . that . . . it was . . . for me. I accept it. I believe."

That was Ben's last message of mercy. He never lived another day. Faith in Christ through the everlasting gospel was his only hope.[1]

That's about the way it is, isn't it?

STEPS TO GROW IN CHRIST

I saw a vibrant Christian friend yesterday, and I said to him, "How are you doing?"

He said, "I'm not. He is."

We've noticed that when a person comes to Christ and gives up on himself (that's *why* he comes), the miracle-working power of the Holy Spirit takes over. In a more supernatural way, it transforms his life, gives him a new heart that leads to a new life. At that point, he is just as saved as he ever will be. Do you believe that? The people who accept what Jesus did on the cross for them, are as saved as they ever will be.

A lifetime of living the Christian life will not add anything to one's salvation. A lifetime with Christ, however, will add a great deal to fellowship and communion and acquaintance and a deepening friendship. Once we come to Christ, what follows then is growth in Christ. Earlier, we explored the steps we take to come *to* Christ. Now we examine the steps we take to grow *in* Christ.

1. PRAYER

The experience "in Christ" begins with prayer. You see, prayer *before* we come to Christ is very different from prayer *after* we come to Christ. Prayer after we have come to Christ becomes personal, one-to-one communication, and its primary purpose is just that.

As you look for a definition of prayer, I think you will discover that most Christians have the idea that the primary purpose of prayer is to get answers from God. I disagree. If prayer is primarily about getting answers, then I am going to pray or not pray in proportion to my answers or lack of answers.

Let's go back to marriage. Why do I talk to my wife? If my marriage disintegrates into talking to my wife only when I need something—"Where is my dinner?" "Where is my ironed shirt?" "Did you wash my socks?" "Will you sew on this button?"—it won't be long before my marriage is kaput.

The primary purpose of communication in marriage is not to get anything; it is to give something that means a lot to two people who are in love. At the heart of the marriage relationship is communication for communication's sake. And isn't that the kind of thing that goes on when you really love someone? You talk for the sake of talking.

My wife and I talk about the same things, over and over and over again. Cherié has never said to me, "Come on, Karl, you know we talked about this very thing six years ago. Isn't there anything else on your agenda? Must we go over the same ground again and again and again?" Actually, we often revisit familiar ground in our conversations. We enjoy talking for talking's sake.

It just so happens that if my primary purpose for communication in my marriage is to communicate for communication's sake, then the rest of the things I need are going to be taken care of. If a button pops off my suit jacket and assaults an unsuspecting saint in the pew (like it did one morning in church!) and my communication with Cherié is good, then all I have to do is walk by her so she can see it, and she'll fix it. If our communication is not good, then I can walk by her all day long, and she'll never notice it.

So the primary purpose of prayer is not to get something. Although the Bible clearly teaches that asking is a piece of prayer. "Ask and it will be given to you," Jesus said, "seek and you will find; knock and the door will be opened to you. For everyone who asks receives; the one who seeks finds; and to the one who knocks, the door will be opened" (Matthew 7:7, 8). God will give us answers, and He invites us to pray for answers, but getting what we want is never to be the primary purpose of prayer. No! Prayer is chiefly for fellowship.

2. Repentance

The next step in Christ is repentance. To many, this is surprising because it is often believed that repentance is the thing we do to come to Christ, not the step we take in Christ. Ellen White clarifies this:

> [Genuine] repentance . . . is beyond the reach of our own power to accomplish; it is obtained only from Christ, who ascended up on high and has given gifts unto men.
>
> Just here is a point on which many may err, and hence they fail of receiving the help that Christ desires to give them. They think that they cannot come to Christ unless they first repent, and that repentance prepares for the forgiveness of their sins. It is true that repentance does precede the forgiveness of sins; for it is only the broken and contrite heart that will feel the need of a Saviour. But must the sinner wait till he has repented before he can come to Jesus? Is repentance to be made an obstacle between the sinner and the Saviour?
>
> The Bible does not teach that the sinner must repent before he can heed the invitation of Christ, "Come unto Me, all ye that labor and are heavy-laden, and I will give you rest." Matthew 11:28. It is the virtue that goes forth from Christ, that leads to genuine repentance. Peter made the matter clear in his statement to the Israelites when he said, "Him hath God exalted with His right hand to be a Prince and a Saviour, for to give repentance to Israel, and forgiveness of sins." Acts 5:31. We can no more repent without the Spirit of Christ to awaken the conscience than we can be pardoned without Christ.
>
> Christ is the source of every right impulse. He is the only one that can implant in the heart enmity against sin. Every desire for truth and purity, every conviction of our own sinfulness, is an evidence that His Spirit is moving upon our hearts.[2]

Repentance is a gift of God, nurtured only by an ongoing, growing relationship with Him. Repentance is not so much something we do as it is something we can't help doing when we really come to Christ. We do not repent in order to come to Christ. It is impossible for us to repent apart from Christ. Repentance is a gift that is given to us after we come to Christ.

Repentance is being sorry that we have disappointed a person, not simply being sorry that we have broken a cold tablet of stone. Genuine, godly repentance has to involve a relationship with a person. There is no such thing as genuine repentance without the warm heart beating in the chest of a person, because repentance is being sorry you have disappointed and let down your best friend.

Have you ever had a good friend whom you inadvertently or deliberately disappointed? Then you realized what it did to him or her, and it broke your heart? This is what repentance is all about.

John Greenleaf Whittier provides a picture of this in his poem, "In School-Days." He tells of an old-fashioned spelling bee in which the girl outlasted the boy that she liked. Thus, she was heartbroken. Then one day after school, she repented. Of course, she did nothing wrong. Winning a spelling contest requires no confession. And her apology is not what we typically classify as "repentance." But she felt compelled just the same, because it affected what really mattered, that is, their friendship. Listen to the ending of his story:

> He saw her lift her eyes; he felt
> The soft hand's light caressing,
> And heard the tremble of her voice,
> As if a fault confessing.
>
> "I'm sorry that I spelt the word:
> I hate to go above you,
> Because,"—the brown eyes lower fell,—
> "Because, you see, I love you!"
>
> Still memory to a gray-haired man
> That sweet child-face is showing.
> Dear girl! the grasses on her grave
> Have forty years been growing!
>
> He lives to learn, in life's hard school,
> How few who pass above him
> Lament their triumph and their loss,
> Like her,—because they love him.[3]

Sorry? Why? Because of a friend. That is repentance.

3. CONFESSION

After repentance, then confession makes sense. But it is not now righteousness by confession like we used to know, where we sit down and take inventory, making lists, and checking them twice, making sure that we have covered everything. *"Ooooooh,"* we stew. "I hope I didn't forget something. I don't want any of these sins to torture me during the time of trouble. I must have a list that's adequate." And so we make our lists and our phone calls and our letters, and we chew our nails and we worry—righteousness by confession.

Instead, now we discover that the Holy Spirit is the Specialist in charge of the confession department. As we come into a close relationship with God and with heaven, the Holy Spirit convicts us about what to do and what not to do in the realm of confession and restitution. Of this we can be absolutely certain: "If we confess our sins, he is faithful and just and will forgive us our sins and purify us from all unrighteousness" (1 John 1:9).

4. Obedience

Further in 1 John, the apostle writes, "We know that we have come to know him if we keep his commands. Whoever says, 'I know him,' but does not do what he commands is a liar, and the truth is not in that person. But if anyone obeys his word, love for God is truly made complete in them. This is how we know we are in him: Whoever claims to live in him must live as Jesus did" (1 John 2:3–6).

As we mature in Christ, obedience naturally follows. Obedience is not something we do to come to Christ; it is a gift that is given to us. Another name for it is, of course, righteousness, the *gift* of righteousness. We obey solely in our absolute dependence upon God. We obey, not because we try hard to obey, but because we would have to try hard not to obey.

For those who have been trying hard all their lives to live by principles and uphold the standards and obey all the rules and to shun all evils to build a perfect character so Jesus can hurry up and come already, listen to this message from Ellen White:

> All true obedience comes from the heart. It was heart work with Christ. And if we consent, He will so identify Himself with our thoughts and aims, so blend our hearts and minds into conformity to His will, that when obeying Him we shall be but carrying out our own impulses. The will, refined and sanctified, will find its highest delight in doing His service. When we know God as it is our privilege to know Him, our life will be a life of continual obedience. Through an appreciation of the character of Christ, through communion with God, sin will become hateful to us.[4]

Have you heard of impulsive obedience? Do you have it? Would you like it? "The will, refined and sanctified, will find its highest delight in doing [God's] service." If that is true, will we have to try hard to obey? Actually, we would have to try hard *not* to obey.

"When we know God as it is our privilege to know Him, our life will be a life of continual [impulsive] obedience. Through an appreciation of the character of Christ, through communion with God, sin will become hateful to us." If sin was hateful to me, would I have to try hard not to sin? No! I would have to try hard to sin!

Suppose we're all in church and I am preaching away on this point of impulsive obedience and the repulsiveness of sin when I pass around a bucket and ask every person in the congregation to spit in it. The bigger the loogie, the better. So the bucket comes by your pew and you oblige with your offering.

When the bucket is overflowing, I hand it to you. It spills on your Sabbath suit. This ticks you off. Not because you have the saints' spittle on your clothes, but because you wanted to drink the whole bucket.

Are you thoroughly disgusted with this illustration? I would hope so! I would not need to tell you not to ingest the saliva. Nor would you be tempted to drink it. Right? Why? Because it would be hateful to you. You would impulsively obey my command not to drink it.

As you come to know and love Jesus Christ as an intimate and personal Friend, anything you might do to sabotage that friendship is as disgusting to you as is the idea of chugging down a community bowl of spit. You won't even be tempted. And your obedience will be impulsive, because of your loyalty to your Friend. Nurturing that friendship will naturally be all consuming.

"But wait a second," someone objects. "This kind of impulsive, natural obedience comes only to super old people after a lifetime of working on the obedience thing. Hopefully, it happens on that one perfect day you will live before you die. Meanwhile, before a person achieves this crowning act of perfection and sanctification, you'd better try hard. Work at it. Work at it. Work at it."

No. I'd argue that God has only one kind of obedience—genuine obedience. It is impulsive, natural, and authentic. And it always and only flows out of an intimate connection with Jesus. Any other flavor of obedience is a ruse.

5. WITNESS

The final reality that happens in Christ is witness. Witnessing becomes spontaneous instead of forced and programmed. Ellen White explains it this way:

> No sooner does one come to Christ than there is born in his heart a desire to make known to others what a precious friend he has found in Jesus; the saving and sanctifying truth cannot be shut up in his heart. If we are clothed with the righteousness of Christ and are filled with the joy of His indwelling Spirit, we shall not be able to hold our peace. If we have tasted and seen that the Lord is good we shall have something to tell.[5]

Authentic Christian witness is when, because we have come into a personal fellowship with the Lord Jesus, we cannot keep quiet. We cannot hold our peace. Like the demon-possessed man who found wholeness and healing in Jesus, we will go to our friends and "tell them how much the Lord has done" (Mark 5:19).

Evangelism, then, is not about out-arguing people on points of doctrine; nor is it about convincing people that your interpretation of the Bible is superior to theirs. Too often, I fear, we talk in the church about witnessing as if we're trying to build our downline business in some elaborate multilevel marketing scheme. Such an approach is sleazy.

I prefer a different approach to evangelism: it is simply one friend telling another friend about a Friend.

Suppose a stranger calls you and says, "You need to change your Internet provider and I'm the guy to do it for you." How likely is it that you'll sign up on the spot? Or suppose somebody you've never met approaches you and says, "I know the person you should marry. He's my nephew. I've set up a blind date for the two of you this Saturday night—the day he gets out of jail. You can trust me. He's the one for you." Are you likely to bite?

Generally speaking, we don't let strangers control the things that matter most to us: our finances, our future, our relationships. Instead, we listen to people we trust. Friends influence friends. If this is true in general, then it's especially true when it comes to the ultimate issue in life—a person's spiritual destiny.

That's how evangelism happens. As you enjoy intimacy with Jesus as a Friend, it is only natural that you introduce Him to your friends. *Think matchmaker, not salesperson.*

If people are going to be reached for Christ, it probably won't happen because of televangelists in white suits screaming about "Gaaawd!" Nor will they be reached primarily through mass mailings of brochures that picture garish beasts with ten heads. Street preachers barking at unknown pedestrians won't finish the work. People will be reached, primarily, through friends.

In the end, a life with God is simply the natural, unforced give-and-take of a close, personal friendship. It starts with communication, that is, prayer. It grows through repentance, when we are honest about how our actions too often damage the relationship. Next, through confession, we seek to strengthen our connection to Christ—dumping those things that would damage the friendship. And while obedience is traditionally positioned as a requirement for the followers of Christ, with this in-Christ approach to faith, obedience is no longer something we muster up the willpower to pull off; instead, it is something we do naturally as it fosters a friendship with Jesus. Only then—when we are engaged in this union with Jesus—are we equipped and motivated to share the good news with others.

THE CLASSROOM

FIRST-GRADE ART

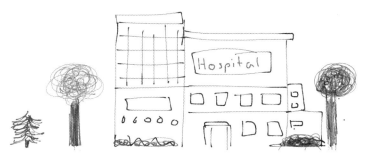

SECOND-GRADE COMPUTERS

 I typed "Jesus" on my Pinterest page, and here's the first board that popped up:

Yep, that says it all. "Know this: my God will also fill every need you have according to His glorious riches in Jesus the Anointed, our Liberating King" (Philippians 4:19, *The Voice*).

Third-Grade Bible

"Whatever I have, wherever I am, I can make it through anything in the One who makes me who I am" (Philippians 4:13, *The Message*).

"All of my spiritual life—I'm talking about the praying, the repenting, the confessing, the obeying, and the witnessing—the whole shebang is only because of my best Friend, Jesus, living in me" (Philippians 4:13, our paraphrase).

Fourth-Grade Writing

Anne Lamott writes, "Grace means you're in a different universe from where you had been stuck, when you had absolutely no way to get there on your own."

Fifth-Grade Math

Jesus + 0 = Salvation

Endnotes

1. Bill Gravestock, "The Everlasting Gospel and Ben Trying," *Present Truth Magazine* 19, accessed August 22, 2013, http://www.presenttruthmag.com/archive/XIX/19-2.htm. Reprinted by permission of the author.

2. Ellen G. White, *Steps to Christ*, 25, 26.

3. John Greenleaf Whittier, "In School-Days," Poetry Foundation, accessed October, 22, 2013, http://www.poetryfoundation.org/poem/174755.

4. Ellen G. White, *The Desire of Ages*, 668.

5. White, *Steps to Christ*, 78.

- 7 -

SPIRITUAL FAILURE FOR DUMMIES

How would you like to be in a profession in which it is your job to tell people how they ought to behave? All the while knowing that you so often fail to live up to the very principles you preach? How would you like my job? Every week I speak to saints and say things such as, "You ought to be kind and tenderhearted toward your spouse"—knowing that I am not always that way toward my wife.

Once Cherié and I were having a major disagreement. I got so angry I slammed the phone down on the carpet. As it bounced off the floor, it rang! So here we are screaming at each other, "Well, if you had done this . . ." and "If only you hadn't done that . . ." when we hear *Riiinnnnggg!*

"Helllllo," I instantaneously went into my pastor's syrupy drawl as I answered the phone. Inevitably, it was a distressed church member who said, "Pastor, my spouse and I are having problems in our marriage. We need your counsel."

I wanted to reply, "I got my own marital woes." A word of advice: Don't call your pastor when he's in the middle of a fight with his wife. It's rude!

I often feel painfully inadequate to tell anybody how they ought to behave. For I know the darkness in my own soul. I get glimpses of my own shadowy choices and twisted motives.

But today I write with great confidence because I'm sharing a topic that I know all about—spiritual failure. I've experienced it enough to speak with authority.

The principles flow out of a story you probably never learned in kindergarten. Let's go back to a time after the nation of Israel split. Israel, the northern kingdom, was ruled by King Ahab; Judah, the southern kingdom, was ruled by King Jehoshaphat.

Our story begins as a young man named Jehoram approaches his father, King Jehoshaphat. The son reports, "Dad, I'm in love."

"With whom?" Jehoshaphat wonders.

Jehoram squirms, for he knows his father will not approve. "Well, Dad, um, ah, I'm in love with King Ahab's daughter, Athaliah."

"Now hold on, Jehoram, you know you can't be with Athaliah, because her parents believe in Baal. We worship Jehovah. God cannot bless any alliance with Baal worshipers."

"But Dad—"

"No! It would dishonor God."

Over and over, Jehoram pleads his case. Finally, Jehoshaphat crumples under the pressure and allows his son to marry the daughter of King Ahab and Queen Jezebel.

Soon Ahab sends an invitation to Jehoshaphat, "Please, come to Samaria to celebrate the newly formed alliance between Israel and Judah."

"Alliance!" Jehoshaphat explodes. "I knew it would come to this." And yet, he gathers his family and his entourage, and he goes to Samaria anyway, even though he knows this to be an act of defiance against God.

Point 1: Go where you don't belong

First, you want to be a spiritual failure? Go where you don't belong. In other words, just leave the Father back at home and go your own way. Remember, faith is all about a relationship with the Father. Sin is severing that intimate connection. So if you want to muff things up, then split from Jesus and go where you don't want Him to go. If your struggle is gambling, just go hang out in Vegas for a weekend. If your temptation is booze, attend a party where you know there will be liquor. If your battle is pornography, get online with no accountability to anyone. It's just a matter of time, and you'll sink. Go where you know you will be tempted.

Jehoshaphat had no business visiting Ahab, yet he went to Samaria anyway. Picture the scene: Ahab's feast takes place on the threshing floor. This is a large flat area used at harvesttime. For example, the laborers would take wheat and pile it on the threshing floor. After horses stomped on it, they would take large trays and start throwing the wheat into the air. If the wind was right, the chaff would float away, leaving just the kernels of wheat.

But on this day, there are no horses, no harvest, and no wheat. The threshing floor is covered with exquisite rugs that bedazzle the senses. It is a football field of color. There is ample drinking, dancing, and feasting on food that has been offered to Baal.

As the evening wears on, Ahab corners Jehoshaphat. "You are a great king," he coos. "I'm so glad my daughter married your son, Jehoram. He is a fine boy," Ahab laid it on real thick.

Point 2: Listen to Satan's flatteries and entertain the thought of compromise

Now we come to our second guideline for spiritual flunkies. If you want to fail, just give an ear to the evil one. Nurse the notions that he plants in your mind:

"I can resist this time."

"What would it be like to sleep with her?"

"I would never get involved in a shady scheme like that."

Just think about it, for the landscape of the spiritual battle is the mind. The key to a robust, healthy spiritual life is staying connected in your thoughts to your Friend, Jesus. Let your mind veer off, and your body is prone to go there. Here is where Jehoshaphat takes the second step toward disaster: he doesn't flee. Instead, he listens to Ahab's twaddle.

Soon Ahab gets to his real agenda. "Jehoshaphat," he says, "do you remember the city of Ramoth Gilead?"

"You mean the city captured by the Syrians? What about it?"

"I want it back," Ahab growls. "Since I don't have the military power to reclaim it by myself, I was thinking we could combine armies and take it back."

Jehoshaphat fidgets. "Well, um, do you have a prophet of whom we might inquire as to whether or not this is God's will?"

Ahab is ready for the objection. He calls Zedekiah, the chief of the four hundred prophets of Baal. They huddle in the middle of the threshing floor. I can imagine some rookie prophet in the circle asking, "So what are we going to tell the king?"

"What do you think?" Zedekiah barks. "We will tell him exactly what he is paying us to say. If we don't, we'll get our heads chopped off. Now make it look like we are praying to Yahweh for an answer."

Finally, Zedekiah steps forward wearing an ox head with iron horns. In melodramatic fashion, he dances before the thrones and shouts, "Go, . . . for God will give it into the king's hand" (2 Chronicles 18:5).

Ahab looks excitedly to Jehoshaphat. "Surely four hundred prophets of God can't be wrong. Are you ready to join armies and reclaim Ramoth Gilead?"

Jehoshaphat squirms. He knows this is not God's will, no matter what the "prophets" may say. So he asks Ahab, "You got any other prophets we could ask?"

"Well, yes," Ahab admits, "there is one other guy. But I don't like him, because he always prophesies evil against me."

"That's the one I'd like to hear from."

So Ahab summons Micaiah, the prophet of the Living God. The messenger offers Micaiah a tip as they're approaching the two kings: "Tell Ahab what he wants to hear."

But Micaiah will not compromise. He informs Ahab's puppet messenger, "I can tell him only what my God says" (verse 13). Oh, how the world is hungry for more Micaiahs—brave men and women who will not be bought or sold.

Micaiah arrives on the scene. He is repulsed by the music, the dancing, the food offered to idols. He knows that Jehoshaphat has no business being in town. He strides toward the throne. King Ahab explains, "King Jehoshaphat and I have decided that we are going to go up and fight to reclaim Ramoth Gilead. Surely this is God's will, is it not?"

Micaiah reads the sham for what it is. Toying with the king like a cat pawing a mouse before the kill, he scoffs, "Sure, go ahead. Combine your armies and you'll live happily ever after. Post a picture on Facebook from your victory party."

But Ahab knows that Micaiah is mocking him. What happens next is like a scene out of a Hollywood blockbuster. Ahab demands, "Tell me the truth!"

"You can't *haaaaandle* the truth," Micaiah retorts. "You want the truth? Here's the truth: you go into battle, and as sure as there is a Living God, you will not return from battle."

Zedekiah goes crazy with rage. "Then Zedekiah son of Kenaanah went up and slapped Micaiah in the face. 'Which way did the spirit from the LORD go when he went from me to speak to you?' he asked" (verse 23).

Ahab is incensed as well. He demands that Micaiah be put in solitary confinement with "nothing but bread and water until I return safely" (verse 26). I can imagine Ahab pointing his bony finger and adding a final jab, "And mark my words, Micaiah, I *will* return safely."

It's the only time Micaiah is mentioned in Scripture. He was a great prophet who was not afraid to speak the truth to power.

After this whole debacle, Ahab turns to Jehoshaphat and says, "So are you ready to go into battle with me?" And even though Jehoshaphat knows beyond any whisper of doubt that this is not God's will, he turns to Ahab and replies, "Sure, let's go to war against Syria."

POINT 3: REFUSE TO OBEY THE CLEARLY REVEALED WILL OF GOD

As a pastor on a university campus, I have seen a steady stream of young people parade through my office, asking the same question: "How do I know God's will?" Somewhere in the conversation, I will often confess, "In my spiritual walk, it's usually not the parts of the Bible where it is difficult to understand God's will that I struggle most with. Most of the time, I know God's will. I just don't want to do it. I know it's God's will for me to be kind, to nurture pure thoughts, to give generously—or whatever the case may be. I know God's will. I just don't do it."

I'm also inclined to explain that rather than asking, "How can I know God's will?" a better question is, "How can I know God?" As I nurture that relationship with God, He leads me. So at the core of spiritual failure is a heart that is estranged from Jesus. The genesis of sin is wandering away from His presence.

If you want to be a spiritual failure, then go against the clearly revealed will of God, which is always to know Him, personally and passionately. Never mind the occasions when God's will is hazy and you genuinely can't discern His leading. Just disregard the teachings of Scripture that are clear, and you'll stumble every time.

Have you ever looked the devil in the eye and said, "Let's dance"? That's what Jehoshaphat did.

The next morning, the Judean and Israelite armies join forces. When Ahab arrives, however, Jehoshaphat is confused. Ahab is not styling in his royal, scarlet robe; he's dressed, instead, like a peasant. Jehoshaphat wants to know what's up with the threads.

Ahab answers, "I have an idea. If you go into battle in your royal chariot, dressed as a king, it will be a decoy. The Syrians will come after you, and then I can ambush them from their blind side."

Amazingly, Jehoshaphat agrees to Ahab's battle plan! What he doesn't know, however, is that "the king of [Syria] had ordered his chariot commanders, 'Do not fight with anyone, small or great, except the king of Israel' " (verse 30). The sole focus of the Syrian soldiers was to capture King Ahab.

So let's go to the battle. Jehoshaphat's army marches over the hill and stampedes into the valley outside of Ramoth Gilead. When the Syrians see the royal chariot, they assume it is Ahab, and they attack.

In a flash, the Syrians surround Jehoshaphat. The Syrian soldiers encircle him. He has a 360-degree view of arrows pointed at his head. Suddenly, Jehoshaphat feels like he is starring in the old Southwest Airlines commercial: "Need to get away?"

But there is nothing Jehoshaphat can do except turn to God. He prays, "Oh Jehovah. Forgive me. I have sinned. I have left Your presence and persued my own follies. I listened to the devil's flatteries and entertained the thought of compromise. Then I disobeyed Your clearly revealed will. Now I am about to die at the hand of our enemy. Jehovah is my God."

The Syrians are confused. "Did he cry out to Jehovah? This can't be Ahab."

The Bible records, "But someone drew his bow at random and hit the king of Israel between the breastplate and the scale armor" (verse 33). King Ahab is wounded. So they prop him up to watch the battle unfold that day. He watches one of the worst massacres in the history of God's people. The Bible records, "All day long the battle raged, and the king of Israel propped himself up in his chariot facing the [Syrians] until evening. Then at sunset he died" (verse 34).

What a dismal chapter in Jehoshaphat's life! Ramoth Gilead remained under Syrian control, and Jehoshaphat gained some valuable insights into how to be a spiritual failure.

LESSONS LEARNED

Do you suppose he learned his lesson? What can we learn from Jehoshaphat's mistakes?

Flipping ahead a couple of chapters, we find the story continues. "After this, the Moabites and Ammonites with some of the Meunites came to wage war against Jehoshaphat. Some people came and told Jehoshaphat, 'A vast army is coming against you from Edom' " (2 Chronicles 20:1, 2). Now keep in mind what had just happened to Jehoshaphat. He had engaged in a war against the will of God. The result was catastrophic. So now Jehoshaphat's military advisers report that neighboring nations are baiting God's people into war. But before Jehoshaphat goes prancing willy-nilly onto the battlefield again, he calls a time-out. This time he sincerely wants to know God's will, and he is determined to follow it. And so, he engages in the practices that will enable him to know God.

So Jehoshaphat declares a fast for all of Judah. Then he addresses the assembly gathered at the temple in Jerusalem and prays this prayer:

> "Lord, the God of our ancestors, are you not the God who is in heaven? You rule over all the kingdoms of the nations. Power and might are in your hand, and no one can withstand you. Our God, did you not drive out the inhabitants of this land before your people Israel and give it forever to the descendants of Abraham your friend? They have lived in it and have built in it a sanctuary for your Name, saying, 'If calamity comes upon us, whether the sword of judgment, or plague or famine, we will stand in your presence before this temple that bears your Name and will cry out to you in our distress, and you will hear us and save us" (verses 6–9).

Jehoshaphat promises God that no matter what happens, he is committed to standing in God's presence. Through calamity, judgment, plague, or famine, Jehoshaphat promises God, "We will stand in your presence." He then concludes the prayer in this way: "We have no power to face this vast army that is attacking us. We do not know what to do, but our eyes are on you" (verse 12).

That's a great prayer to recite when facing temptation or seeking to know God's will. Use Jehoshaphat's prayer: "I do not know what to do, but my eyes are upon You."

Following this season of fasting and prayer, God delivers His answer through the prophet Jahaziel. Verse 15 records this message: "Listen, King Jehoshaphat and all who live in Judah and Jerusalem! This is what the Lord says to you: 'Do not be afraid or discouraged because of this vast army. For the battle is not yours, but God's.' " I know of no principle more important than this one when it comes to gaining spiritual victory. Never forget: "The battle is not yours, but God's."

Too often we approach spiritual life like an assignment to keep a hundred beach balls submerged in the Pacific Ocean at the same time. If you're a strong swimmer, you may keep a ball under water with your feet and a couple more submerged with your hands, but soon you'll feel defeated and exhausted.

Similarly, some people think, *If I can just keep my sins—my pride and gluttony and lust—under the surface so others don't see them, then maybe I'll at least appear holy.* Mark my words, soon you will feel defeated and exhausted.

So what's the answer? The answer is to get out of the water and into the boat with Jesus. The key is not to try harder to be good; rather, it is to remain in the presence of Jesus. For you see, sin and Jesus cannot coexist in the same heart. Remember, "the battle is not yours, but God's." Your battle is to remain always in the presence of God in order to let His life be willed through you. In this way, victory occurs before temptation, when you are experiencing His presence and surrendering yourself fully to Him.

It's like the father who tells of watching his three-year-old daughter fight the temptation of the cookie jar. The girl doesn't notice that her father is watching from a distance. So she climbs a shelf in the pantry and stretches to snitch a snack. Now she knows the cookie jar is off limits. Her spirit wants to resist temptation, but her flesh craves a sugar hit. Just as she grabs a cookie, Dad clears his throat. Instantly, she drops the cookie and scoots away.

Think about it: one moment, the kid could not resist temptation, but in an instant, she models the resolution of a saint. What made the difference? It's simple. It was the presence of her father.

Our battles with temptation work the same way with the notable exception, of course, that our motive is never fear (as one might argue in the case of the cookie-snatching kid) but love. We never want to disappoint our Friend. In our own strength, the flesh always wins. But when we live in the presence of our heavenly Father, we are then positioned to allow God to fight the battle for us.

Thomas Kelly put it this way: "Don't grit your teeth and clench your fists and say, 'I will! I will!' Relax. Take hands off. Submit yourself to God. Learn to live in the passive voice—a hard saying for Americans—and let life be willed through you."[1]

That's precisely what the Judeans did. This time, rather than some strategy to trick the enemy by dressing the king like a peasant, Jehoshaphat gave up trying to figure out how he would win the war. He let God fight the battle for him. He focused on spiritual training through the disciplines of fasting, prayer, and corporate worship. In fact, the forces of Judah approached war as an act of corporate worship, singing the hymn "Give thanks to the LORD, for his love endures forever" (verse 21). In the end, victory is not about trying, nor is it just about training. It is all about trusting the battle to God.

When the army of Jehoshaphat reached the battlefield, they were stunned by what they saw. Their enemies had turned on themselves! The Judean soldiers stood on the bluff overlooking a valley of corpses. God had already arrived to conquer the enemy on their behalf.

The Bible records, "There was so much plunder that it took three days to collect it. On the fourth day they assembled in the Valley of Berakah, where they praised the LORD" (verses 25, 26).

Jehoshaphat learned that the battle indeed belongs to the Lord. You see, God loves us so much that He takes the responsibility of transforming us into His character.

The children's book *Little Lord Fauntleroy* helps to illustrate what we're talking about. It tells the story of a seven-year-old boy who went to stay with his grandpa. Although the grandpa had a reputation of being extremely mean and selfish, the lad took a great interest in him. Over and over, the boy complimented his grandpa, finding only positive things to say about him.

"Oh, Grandpa," he gushed, "how people must love you! You're so good and kind." No matter how disagreeable the elderly man was, the grandson saw the best in everything grandpa did.

Finally, the youngster's unquestioning love softened the heart of the cantankerous old man. Grandpa couldn't resist the unwavering trust that the boy had in his goodness. As a result, he gradually began to change his ways, and, in time, he became the unselfish and kind person his grandson thought him to be.

Although it's a make-believe kid's tale, it does capture the true story of us all. From God's perspective, we offer Him little to love. Nevertheless, God takes a great interest in us. Scripture tells us, "But God demonstrates his own love for us in this: While we were still sinners, Christ died for us" (Romans 5:8).

You don't have to clean up your act for God to love you. No need to go to church or memorize Leviticus or kick that nasty habit or buy a Bible. Every splinter of the cross screams of God's unquestioning love.

You are good enough just the way you are for God to love you. But God loves you too much to let you stay the way you are.

Like the grandpa in *Little Lord Fauntleroy,* you and I can change. We can become unselfish and kind—just like Jesus! Now mind you, this change does not occur by trying hard to change. That's as fruitless and frustrating as trying to get a tan in a dark room by gritting your teeth and clenching your fists and chanting, "I *will* get a suntan!"

How often do we fight temptation by that method of trying a little harder? "I will not take a drink." "I will not gossip." "I will not eat that pie." "I will not . . ." It's much simpler. To tan, live in the sun.

Similarly, to overcome sin, live in the *Son.* Don't waste your time trying to be holy. Instead, live in the presence of He who is holy. Then, as you live in the security of God's unconditional love, He will fight your battles, and you will be changed into His likeness.

THE CLASSROOM

FIRST-GRADE ART

SECOND-GRADE COMPUTERS

Google "spiritual failure" and one of the 25,700 hits will take you to a Web site that gives this counsel from Glynnis Whitwer: "So today if you feel like a spiritual failure, read Romans 2. There's some hope in there for us today."[2]

THIRD-GRADE BIBLE

"Do not be afraid or discouraged. . . . For the battle is not yours, but God's" (2 Chronicles 20:15).

God: "What's your battle? The bottle? The Internet? The rage? The gossip? The soaps? Here's some good news: You don't have to live in fear anymore. Don't be discouraged when you cave in to that same old sin. Let Me fight the battle for you. Stop trying. Start trusting. And you will experience deliverance. I promise" (2 Chronicles 20:15, our paraphrase).

Fourth-Grade Writing

On page 132 of *Reflecting Christ,* Ellen White writes, "Jesus the Son of God humbled Himself for us, endured temptation for us, overcame in our behalf, to show us how we may overcome."

Fifth-Grade Math

Trying ≪ Training < Trusting = Spiritual Formation

Endnotes

1. Thomas R. Kelly, *A Testament of Devotion* (San Francisco: HarperCollins, 1941, 1992), 29.

2. Glynnis Whitwer, "Do You Ever Feel Like a Spiritual Failure?" Glynnis Whitwer, accessed September 1, 2013, http://glynniswhitwer.com/2010/09/do-you-ever-feel-like -spiritual-failure/.

– 8 –

SICK FAITH VERSUS STRONG FAITH

If Morrie Venden's legacy were reduced to a single parable that he told, it would be this signature story:

I heard about this fantastic city. The city is square—over three hundred miles on each side and three hundred miles high as well. It boasts of trees and rivers and streets of gold! There are no cemeteries or tombstones, no hospitals, no broken hearts, and nobody gets old in this city.

I want to go there. So one day I get in my car, and I head down the freeway towards that city. I notice on a road sign that it's 105 trillion miles away. So I step on the gas. If I'm ever to arrive, I'll need to go at least ninety miles an hour.

But the strangest thing happens. I discover shortly after leaving town that most of the traffic is going the other way—against me. And although it is a lovely four-lane highway, there is not a center divider. The traffic all seems to be on my side of the road.

Now I don't like head-on collisions, so I find myself over on the shoulder, driving on gravel. You don't drive ninety miles an hour on the shoulder unless you aspire to be roadkill. So I ease off the gas until I'm putting along at twenty miles an hour, very discouraged. If you're going to drive 105 trillion miles, you've got to do at least ninety.

One day around the bend comes this huge diesel truck. It was a Peterbilt, and this has nothing to do with the Catholics. This truck is loaded with hay. It heads straight for me, puttering along on the shoulder. Before the truck hits me, I go into the ditch—crunching my fender and cracking the windshield.

As I'm sitting there, very discouraged, I begin thinking about that fantastic city. I've got to try again. Step on the gas, out of the ditch, and back up on the shoulder doing twenty.

A few days later, what should appear but another diesel truck! There is a whole fleet of these dumb diesels, this time hauling coal, coming straight at me. Into the ditch I go. Discouraged.

Then I start thinking about that city. Back on the shoulder. Another few days. Another diesel. Back in the ditch.

One day I am sitting there in the ditch, seriously considering giving up on the whole trip, when there is a knock on my window. I am surprised, because I haven't seen any hitchhikers. I look out the window, and there is a man dressed in white. He says, "Do you want me to drive for you?"

"Well," I say, "I've sure been making a mess of it. I'm not getting anywhere."

He says, "I've been over the road."

"You have?"

"Yes."

I throw the door open, and I let him in. I move out of the driver's seat and let him take the steering wheel. He is now in control.

I notice his big, muscular arms. "What kind of work have you been doing?" I ask.

He says, "I've been working in a cabinet shop."

He steps on the gas. Up onto the freeway and straight down the freeway at ninety miles an hour against the traffic. The Datsuns and the Volkswagens and the Lincoln Continentals stay out of his way. I can't believe it. His jaw is set, his eyes are clear. I see something like a smile on his face, and I start laughing. With this man for my driver, there is a chance I can reach the distant city. In fact, I am so excited about my new driver that I want to roll down the window and shout to everyone, "You should see my driver!" I even want a bumper sticker that reads, "Honk if you know my driver."

So we're cruising along, making good time. But I discover that my driver is not pushy. In fact, I have to invite him to stay in the car with me day by day in order for him to continue with me. He is always there, knocking on the door, but I have to open the door and let him in.

One day we are going along the freeway, and around the bend comes another diesel truck. Needless to say, I don't relish the idea of a head-on collision with a truck doing ninety miles an hour. So before we crash, I lunge for the steering wheel. My driver takes his hands off the wheel, and it is completely under my control. I whip the wheel around.

Suddenly, there is screeching of tires, with dust and gravel in the air. The car careens from side to side and finally flies into the ditch. Clearly, the car is totaled—fenders smashed, windows crashed, and axles busted.

When the dust settles, my driver taps me on the shoulder. "Want me to drive again?"

"And how are you going to drive a car in this condition?" I wonder. To my surprise, not only is he a cabinetmaker, but he is an excellent body and fender man as well.

In short order, the wreck is restored, and we're good to go. I ask him to do the driving. He takes the wheel, steps on the gas, and slides back into traffic.

As we're zooming along at ninety miles an hour, I remind myself, *This driver has been over the road before. He told me so. He must know about diesel trucks.* I begin debating with myself what I will do if another diesel truck comes. I am not too pleased with what happened when I grabbed the wheel.

Sure enough, a few days later, around the bend comes another diesel truck, loaded with hay. He heads straight toward us again.

I fasten my seat belt. I chew on my fingernails. I fidget in the seat. I look at my driver. He is as calm as can be. I look at the diesel truck, and panic seizes me. I want to grab the wheel, but I tell myself, "No! Don't do it."

Have you ever heard the expression "Don't just sit there, do something"? This is just the opposite: "Don't do something, just sit there!" We get closer to the diesel. I look at my driver again. He has stepped on the gas and is now going 120. I look at the diesel.

Panic!

I look at my driver. He has a smile on his face.

Just before we collide, the diesel veers off into the ditch. I get a glimpse of the driver of the diesel. He has a pitchfork beside him there in the cab—for loading hay.

Now I am overjoyed. I can't believe it. Not only do the Datsuns and Volkswagens get out of our way, so do the diesel trucks. I am thrilled with my driver. So I say to myself, "Just stay out of the driver's seat. Keep your hands off the steering wheel." But he never takes that power of choice away from me. I can choose one of two things: I can choose not to invite him into the car with me on a daily basis, or I can choose to take control of the steering wheel at any time.

FIGHTING THE FIGHT OF FAITH

Please don't misinterpret the parable to suggest passivity. The Christian life is not passive. Paul counsels Timothy, "Fight the good fight" (1 Timothy 6:12). This suggests action, work, and effort, right? But what is this good fight? Paul calls it the "fight of the faith." To understand the fight of the faith, we must understand what faith is.

Some people say, "Faith is believing." Sure, it could include that. But sometimes faith is the opposite of believing. Another person says, "Faith is taking God at His word." But there are times when faith is the opposite of taking God at His word. Are you aware of that?

Consider the story in Matthew 15. Jesus goes up to the coast of Tyre and Sidon. A woman approaches Him and cries, "Lord, Son of David, have mercy on me! My daughter is demon-possessed and suffering terribly" (verse 22). Notice the sobering response: "Jesus did not answer a word" (verse 23).

In this case, faith could not mean taking God at His word, because there is no word yet. Jesus knew that His disciples were watching Him carefully, because they considered this woman to be a heathen and they weren't supposed to talk to her.

So they urged Jesus, "Send her away" (verse 23).

The woman continued to plead until Jesus said the very thing the disciples would have expected a good Jewish person to say: "I've got my hands full dealing with the lost sheep of Israel" (verse 24, *The Message*).

Have you ever been ignored by someone? Ever gone and talked to someone, and the person turned his back on you? Did you stick around? Or have you ever asked someone for directions or help with homework or something, only to hear "I am not here to help you"? How did you like it?

If faith is about believing what Jesus said or if faith means taking God at His word, this little woman would have been gone long before He got to the good part. But she kept pleading with Him. She said, "Lord, help me!" (verse 25).

Jesus replied, "It is not right to take the children's bread and toss it to the dogs" (verse 26).

Have you ever asked someone for help only to be called a dog? But this little lady was dogged in her determination. She points out that even dogs get the crumbs from the Master's table. You gotta love her comeback: "If I am going to be a dog, then I am entitled to some dog food!" I imagine a twinkle in Jesus' eye as He said to her, " 'Woman, you have great faith! Your request is granted.' And her daughter was healed at that moment" (verse 28).

In this story, faith was not taking Jesus at His word. It was *not* believing what He said. Faith was the opposite of believing what He said. Therefore, the best definition of faith is actually inherent in the Greek root from which the word is translated. It can be translated as "trust."

Ellen White puts it simply, "Faith is trusting God."[1] The woman did not believe what Jesus said. She did not take Him at His word. But she trusted Him.

So if we are going to fight the good fight of faith, let's understand that it is a call to fight the good fight of trust.

To trust somebody, you need two things. First, you have to have someone who is trustworthy. But someone could be ever so trustworthy, and you still wouldn't put your trust there until the second requirement is met. You have to *know* the person, right?

Take the reverse of that. A person can be absolutely untrustworthy, but I will not distrust him until I get to know him. When I get to know him, the distrust will become automatic. The Bible premise is that God is One in whom you can trust. Jesus is absolutely trustworthy. Therefore, the only other thing you need in order to learn to trust Him is to get to know Him. And when you get to know Him, you will trust Him. You won't have to try. You will.

Faith is spontaneous. Faith is never something you work on; nor is it something you work up. Somehow we get this idea that if we can just sort of put ourselves out on a limb and force ourselves into a situation where God will have to work, that this is exercising faith. No! This is presumption—like writing a check from an empty account as an act of believing that God will make a deposit before we go bankrupt.

Some think faith is something you work on—you back up and get a run at it and try to make yourself believe. If you can believe hard enough that something is going to happen, then it will happen. Conversely, if you don't believe hard enough, then God won't act.

Preposterous! That is sick faith.

You don't work on faith. What do you work on? Put your effort into knowing Jesus; if you want to call this a work, OK. When you get acquainted with Jesus, who is absolutely trustworthy, faith comes spontaneously. You trust Him.

Precisely! That is strong faith.

GETTING ACQUAINTED

How do you get acquainted with people? By talking to them, by listening to them talk to you, and by going places and doing things together.

What do we call talking to God? Prayer.

How does God talk to us? Through His Word.

How do we go places and do things together with God? By sharing our faith and serving others in Jesus' name.

Prayer, Bible study, and witness—these are the three legitimate works that produce faith in Christ. (For specific suggestions on how to nurture these "works" in your life, see appendixes A–E.) Without this emphasis on a personal relationship with Jesus, then righteousness by faith becomes cheap grace, for it suggests that all we do is sit in a rocking chair and wait for God to do everything.

We have a part to play. It is the good fight of faith; it is good, but make no mistake, it is a fight. So when we talk about sanctification—this process of being transformed into the likeness and character of Christ—occurring by faith alone, what are we saying? We are suggesting that everything is embodied in that word *faith.*

In other words, it is sanctification by relationship with Christ alone. Transformation and victory over sin occur only through a continuing fellowship and communication with Christ. Period! When we say "sanctification by faith alone" (assuming a correct understanding of what genuine faith is), we don't have to get nervous about rocking-chair religion. For genuine faith demands action, and such action is always aimed at getting acquainted with God. Focus only, always, consistently on nurturing this relationship, and trust Jesus to tackle your sins.

"My dear children," John says, "I write this to you so that you will not sin. But if anybody does sin, we have an advocate with the Father—Jesus Christ, the Righteous One" (1 John 2:1). Whenever we separate ourselves from God and fail in our own strength, not to worry—we have a Friend who covers us. Our continuing certainty of salvation is unbroken as long as the relationship continues.

Ellen White explains, "If one who daily communes with God errs from the path, if he turns a moment from looking steadfastly unto Jesus, it is not because he sins willfully; for when he sees his mistake, he turns again, and fastens his eyes upon Jesus, and the fact that he has erred does not make him less dear to the heart of God. He knows that he has communion with the Saviour; and when reproved for his mistake in some matter of judgment, he does not walk sullenly, and complain of God, but turns the mistake into a victory."[2]

Growth in the Christian life is learning more and more to distrust our own power and to trust the power of our Redeemer. And all the time that we are learning this, He is patiently guiding us, showing us how to stay out of the driver's seat, teaching us to let Him remain in control in our lives by our choice.

His patience, His kindness, His compassions fail not. The reservoirs of God's grace are inexhaustible for the one who is seeking intimate friendship.

How can you lose? When I look to myself and consider my past record of wrecks, there is not a chance in the world that I can be saved. When I look to Jesus and His might and His mercy and His grace, there's not a chance in the world that I can be lost.

THE CLASSROOM

FIRST-GRADE ART

SECOND-GRADE COMPUTERS

 A prayer posted on the blog site TUMBLR: "Spirit lead me where my trust is without borders; let me walk upon the waters, wherever you would call me; take me deeper than my feet would ever wander" (thestateofunoia).

THIRD-GRADE BIBLE

"You are my little children, so I am writing these things to help you avoid sin. If, however, any believer does sin, we have a high-powered defense lawyer—Jesus the Anointed, the righteous—arguing on our behalf before the Father. It was through His sacrificial death that our sins were atoned. But He did not stop there—He died for the sins of the whole world" (1 John 2:1, 2, *The Voice*).

"OK, kids, listen up! The ideal, of course, is that you're never going to mess up. But let's get real—you will blow it more times than you care to admit. So here's what God did to make it like you've never sinned: He sent His only Son, Jesus Christ, who now stands as your Friend and Attorney, arguing on your behalf before the Judge. Accept the gift of Jesus' death, and you are perfect. He takes your punishment for messing up, and you can have His record of never making a mistake. The whole world can know this guilt-free joy!" (1 John 2:1, 2, our paraphrase).

Fourth-Grade Writing

Eugene Peterson writes, "Everybody treats us so nicely. No one seems to think that we mean what we say. When we say 'kingdom of God,' no one gets apprehensive, as if we had just announced (which we thought we had) that a powerful army is poised on the border, ready to invade. When we say radical things like 'Christ,' 'love,' 'believe,' 'peace,' and 'sin'—words that in other times and cultures excited martyrdoms—the sounds enter the stream of conversation with no more splash than baseball scores and grocery prices" (*Leadership*, vol. 10, no. 2).

Fifth-Grade Math

Strong Faith = (Trust in Self $\times$ 0) + (Trust in God)$^\infty$

Endnotes

1. Ellen White, *Education* (Mountain View, CA: Pacific Press®, 1952), 253.

2. Ellen White, *The Faith I Live By* (Washington, DC: Review and Herald®, 1958), 118.

- 9 -

GROWTH IN GRACE

So we're driving down the freeway, and I'm excited about this trip. My driver is absolutely capable. He's been over the road; he knows about the diesel trucks, the whole bit. And we keep going. Making real time toward that distant city. I can't explain it, but there's this uncanny power that I allow to get through to me from the driver of that diesel truck.

We are going along one day, and up ahead I see, off the road to the left—not the right—an amusement park. Fun! There are certainly more sinister forms of entertainment out there, and I'm in the mood for some fun.

Have you ever noticed the difference between happiness and fun?

Now I am quite sure that my driver is not going to drive down into this amusement park. I have to take the wheel. So I tap my driver on the shoulder and say, "Pardon me, may I drive?"

"Sure. Sure."

He's never pushy. I can drive any time I want to. I always maintain the power of choice. But I had invited him to stay with me in the car that day. And he stays in the car.

I slow down and turn left. There is a hill between the amusement park and us. I come over the rise of the hill, and right down there by the amusement park is a cliff. I don't see it.

Off the cliff we sail.

Down at the bottom of the cliff, as I am stirring from a blackout, my driver is there. "You want me to drive again?" he asks.

I'm not sure what car he's asking to drive. But somehow he puts the totaled wreck back together, and soon enough we're cruising the highway again.

For months, we're clipping along. Then I notice to my amazement that there are times when I unconsciously slip toward the steering wheel. There is something that is strangely attractive about it. Part of it is that, well, I'm a big boy. I know how to drive. I've been to driving school. I have a driver's license. It is ego deflating to admit that I can't drive. There are times when I find myself with my hands on the wheel when I don't even realize it until I see another diesel truck coming.

One day I had my hands on the wheel when a diesel truck barreled around the bend. My first impression was to slide over, give him the wheel—but hey, I had seen the driver enough times. There was no reason I couldn't just do the same thing that he always did. So I kept my hands on the wheel and headed straight for the diesel.

He stepped it up to 120; I stepped it up to 120. I even pushed it to 121—straight for the diesel. I figured, if diesels go in the ditch when he is driving, why not when I am driving?

You know what happened. There was a horrible head-on collision.

And I would have lost my life except for the driver throwing himself in front of me. He was badly broken and bleeding.

Moments later, I heard his kind voice. "Do you want me to drive?"

"Drive what?" I asked.

To my amazement, he pieced the wreck together, and soon we were flying down the road again.

I noticed his bruises and blood. I choked up with sorrow. I was really sorry for what I had done to him. I asked him to forgive me.

The journey isn't over yet. The other day we came to a fork in the road; to the right the pavement ended and turned into gravel and then into a dirt road with chuckholes that wound its way up the side of this mountain.

To the left, the road was a beautiful eight-lane parkway, down through some sunken gardens. Beautiful. Acres and acres of waving palm trees, streams, springs and fountains, golf courses, and lush lawns. I assumed this must be the border of that distant city.

Guess which turn my driver took. The chuckholes! I tapped him on the shoulder and said, "Did you see the other road?"

"Yes."

"Are you on the right road?"

"Yes."

"Are you sure you're on the right road?"

"Do you want me to drive?"

"Well, yes."

He continued to drive, and I noticed that as he came to the chuckholes, he made his way around them as carefully as possible. The farther we got up the side of the mountain, the more I began to see something strange down at the sunken gardens. On the other side of the sunken gardens, huge billows of smoke were rolling up, like the smoke from burning diesel and hay trucks. And I thought, *Yes! He does know the right way; he's been over the road before.*

The farther we got up the side of the mountain, the more I could see a glorious light coming from the other side of the mountain. I thought it might be the light from that city. Just over the mountain in the Promised Land, lies the Holy City built by God's own hand!

Well that's as far as we go with the parable. This is the souped-up version; but if you'd like to read an older version of it, with horse and buggy and mountain road and cliffs, you can read it in *Early Writings* by Ellen White. As she tells it, the story ends with ropes coming down from above, and the travelers finally swing across, totally dependent upon the ropes.

WORKING ON GROWING

As the road trip drags on, there are plenty of distractions that would detour us. But as long as we allow the Driver to drive, we can trust that we are going in the right direction and growing along the way. Yes, I said, *"growing."*

Sometimes people get nervous with the idea of righteousness by faith for fear that it negates growth. After all, if it's all about faith in Jesus, then there are no works, right?

Wrong.

That would be a complete misunderstanding of righteousness by faith, because righteousness by faith is the *only* thing that will produce works. Any works apart from righteousness by faith are not works of authentic righteousness. Growth doesn't happen by focusing hard on growth and trying to grow.

When I was a kid, I wanted to be six feet tall. I don't know why—maybe because I had just read a biography of Abraham Lincoln. But I wasn't doing very well—three feet, eight inches. In fact, I was the shortest kid in my eighth-grade class. When you have to stand in the front row with the girls for your eighth-grade graduation picture, well, that's about as low as a boy can go.

Then I had an idea. I went out and hung on the clothesline post. Before doing so, I had measured myself against the doorjamb so I could check to see how much I had helped conditions.

To my chagrin, it didn't help a bit. But I'm not telling you anything Jesus didn't tell you a long time ago. "Which of you by worrying can add one cubit to his stature?" (Matthew 6:27, NKJV).

You don't grow by trying to grow; you grow by eating. If I had spent all of my time hanging on the clothesline post so that I had no time to come in for dinner, it would be safe to say that I would never have reached six feet tall, only six feet under.

It would be absurd for someone to suggest to me that I am antigrowth because I am not hanging on a clothesline post. No, I am pro-growth, because I am eating. Right here you have the demonstration of the proper operation of the human will in the Christian life.

It's a misuse of your will, your power of choice, and your willpower to put your effort and your choosing toward trying to do something you can't do. The right use of your will, your power to choose, and your willpower is to put your effort and your choice toward doing something you can do, which will result, in turn, in that which you can't do.

I go down to San Francisco to take off for my flight to Chicago. I skip the airport terminal, go out to the end of the runway, and begin flapping my arms in the breeze to take off on my flight to Chicago. I flap my arms in the breeze just as hard as I can until finally someone comes by in a Jeep and asks, "What are you doing?"

"I'm trying to take off for Chicago."

And they say, "We have another place for you to go."

That would be working on something that I cannot achieve. It's a recipe for failure and frustration. But if I choose to place myself in the hands of a pilot onboard a plane bound for Chicago, then I am choosing to do something that will result in me getting to Chicago. And the pilot will get me there.

Once again, this illustration is inadequate because it implies passivity—like I just sit around and do nothing. Please don't take every nuance of the illustration literally. Righteousness by faith does not lead to passivity; it leads me to the highest acts and the greatest works of God that I have ever known. Only, it is God that is in me—motivating and driving me with the power of love. It's surprising how active "passive" can be!

Surrendering my life to the pilot onboard the plane will lead to fantastic activity. In the spiritual realm, surrendering my life to the Pilot will lead me to do things that otherwise I wouldn't enjoy doing and would never be able to do, because it is God who is able to will and do these activities in me.

When David surrendered his life to God and became an instrument in God's hands, he did the impossible and killed Goliath. Jonathan and his armor bearer, totally dependent upon God, did not sit in camp. God motivated them to climb the mountain steep, and these two lone men got a box seat to watch God conquer the enemy.

But it wasn't really two lone men; it was the mighty power of God at work in two men who had surrendered themselves to be totally under God's control.

Again and again as you go through God's Word, you find that whatever you might tend to call passive is extremely active. God wants us to be passive toward fighting the battle where the battle isn't. He wants us to be passive toward hanging on the clothesline post. But He does want us to be active toward the fight of faith—which means eating the bread of life.

How do you grow?

You grow by eating. You grow by breathing. You grow by exercising. You don't grow by trying to grow. No one becomes righteous by trying to be righteous.

Anyone who is ever righteous will be righteous, because he or she has come to know Jesus. You don't have faith by trying to work up faith. Faith is not something you work on; faith comes spontaneously to those who spend their time and energy knowing Jesus. Peter said, "Grow in the grace and knowledge of our Lord and Savior Jesus Christ" (2 Peter 3:18, NKJV). The Bible commands that we *grow*.

Now just because I eat and just because I breathe does not mean I am going to be healthy, but I'm sure not going to be healthy if I don't.

And just because you read your Bible and just because you pray, which is the breath of the soul, doesn't mean that you are going to be spiritually healthy; but you certainly are not going to be if you don't.

It is possible to change Bible study and prayer and the devotional life into a system of works. Instead of not smoking, not drinking, and not dancing, you are putting in your sixty minutes and you are putting in your knee work, and you're getting it done. It can become a system, a routine.

Some people say, "Listen, I've tried the devotional life. I've tried to read my Bible and pray, and it doesn't do anything for me. What shall I do?"

Well, there is one thing not to do. Don't quit. Bailing on building a friendship with Jesus won't help.

Instead go to God. Pour out your need to Him.

Go to another Christian friend and say, "Look, I'm having trouble in my devotional life. Can you give me some help? Will you pray with me?"

You keep exploring and probing until you find meaning in the devotional life. You don't just ditch it because you've tried it for three days and it doesn't seem to be working.

"Oh," you say, "that sounds like work."

Yes, this is the legitimate "work" in the realm of the Christian experience. I believe that it is the one area where it is possible and necessary to put forth real effort. It is, after all, called a fight in the Bible—the fight of faith.

The devil will do everything he can to keep you from eating God's Word, from breathing in prayer, and from exercising in reaching out in service toward others.

TIPS FOR A MEANINGFUL DEVOTIONAL EXPERIENCE

Often I am asked, "How can I have a better devotional life?" My answer is based on the following statement from Jesus: "I am the bread of life. Whoever comes to me will never go hungry, and whoever believes in me will never be thirsty" (John 6:35).

Using this analogy, we see a connection between the physical and the spiritual. How much time do you spend eating your meals day by day? Half an hour? An hour? An hour and a half? Here's a helpful guideline: spend as much time alone with God as you do eating your physical meals.

Is it any wonder that we have this counsel: "It would be well for us to spend a thoughtful hour each day in contemplation of the life of Christ. We should take it point by point, and let the imagination grasp each scene, especially the closing ones."[1]

Now, who does your eating? You do. No one else eats for you; you have to eat for yourselves. No one else can digest your food for you. Family worship is great; public worship is great; but it is no substitute for private worship.

In the eating analogy, we take time to eat, and we do it for ourselves. We feed ourselves; no one else feeds us. Of course, it is nice to eat together, if you are going to follow through on the illustration. But family prayer is no substitute for private prayer. Time alone with God at the beginning of the day can't be replaced by just attending church.

If you want to know a secret for a meaningful devotional life, make time for Jesus first thing in the morning. After the cold shower and after the jogging, if necessary, when our metabolism is in gear. Time alone at the beginning of every day.

We eat every day, usually two or three times a day. No wonder Daniel grew spiritually; he prayed, and he spent time with God three times a day. But at least begin the day with God. Spend time every morning investing in your friendship with Jesus. This time is crucial—not just when the roof is caving in, not just on Sabbath or just when there is a Week of Prayer, but every day should include personal fellowship with God.

And here is another clue: seek Jesus. I believe the most meaningful devotional life is going to focus on the life of Jesus. Then if you have extra time and you want to supplement that with something else, fine, but the bulk of your devotional life is going to be confined to a study of the life of Jesus. Which means what? Well, I recommend reading a book such as *The Desire of Ages*. At the bottom of the first page of most chapters, it says, "This chapter is based on . . ." Read the listed Bible verses and follow with the commentary in the chapter.

There will be times, of course, when your mind wanders. Don't go to the preacher and complain, "The devotional life doesn't work. My mind drifted. I quit." Keep reading. Back up and read it again. Effort? Yes. Legitimate effort.

Bible Study

Another tip: personalize it. As you are reading, don't read the Bible as a history lesson of something that happened more than two thousand years ago. Read it with yourself in the picture.

So when you read about the thief on the cross, instead of thinking about that poor thief out there, suddenly *you* are the thief, and *you* are hanging on the cross. In your imagination, you try to understand what it would have been like to be there. As the thief, you remember that you have heard of Jesus before this moment. You have perhaps even been somewhere in the crowd at arm's length when Jesus was speaking or healing, and you have been impressed by what you have heard of Him, how He accepts everyone.

He accepts sinners and harlots and thieves and Pharisees. Anyone who will come to Him, He always accepted. He heals lepers, the untouchables; He opens the eyes of blind people; He raises the dead. He has talked about His eternal kingdom, and as you are hanging there on the cross, just about ready to kiss life goodbye, it suddenly floods into you that this Man might accept you too!

And you say, "Lord, remember me."

And just like that He says, "You are going to be with Me in heaven."

Fantastic? Absolutely! If Jesus can treat a poor thief like that, then He can do something for me as well.

PRAYER

Find yourself in the story. As you do this, carry on a conversation with Jesus. For example, you're reading Mark 15 about Simon from Cyrene. You hear the soldiers mocking Jesus. You smell the torches. You see the cobblestones and shrubbery. You feel the splinters as they thrust that cross on your shoulders. As you are engaging your senses in the story, you pray, "God, I've been reading today about Simon. The text says, 'They forced him to carry the cross' (verse 21). He didn't necessarily want to carry it, but he obviously had a soft spot in his heart for Jesus and was grateful for the opportunity. Please put Your cross on my shoulders today."

Talk to Jesus in this way. When you have talked to Him and asked Him to take your life for that day, you wait. Don't go racing off to post something on Instagram or to exercise the dog.

Wait.

Shut your mouth.

Listen.

God may have something to say to you—not in an audible voice but through impressions in your mind. I believe God will often guide your thoughts while you are praying if you will give Him a chance. It's a two-way conversation.

If you have never had a meaningful devotional life before, you might find it hard to get into it. Give God a chance. That is the only way you will grow in grace.

OUTREACH

There is one other ingredient to growth: witness or sharing or service. Right away people say, "Oh, no, please not that. Ringing doorbells! Oh, deliver me."

I used to do that as a pastor; I would fake it. This is one of the things that gave me ulcers the first couple of years in ministry. I felt forced to press my congregation. "This afternoon we have the opportunity to go out and share our faith," I'd say, trying to pump up the saints. All the while I was thinking, *There's nothing I hate more than "witnessing."* Then I would go down the street and ring doorbells of people I had never seen before. Housewives would come to the door, and I would say, "I just came by to get acquainted."

They would say, "I beg your pardon?"

Jesus didn't tell us to go out to strangers primarily. Do you know what He said to the average follower? He told the person to go and share what the Lord had done personally in his or her life.

Away with this idea that you have to go to the gutter and rescue the drunk in order to be involved in witnessing. Go to the person across the hall. Learn from the woman at the well and ask for a cup of cold water. Reverse the process and say, "I've been watching you. Would you please tell me what Jesus means to you?" No one will charge you with cramming religion down their throat with this approach.

One of the greatest things that ever happened to me was when I went out one night and asked some friends, "Please, will you tell me what Jesus means to you? What He has done for you?" Often they were looking for a chance to share. By doing this, I was able to learn vicariously what it means to come into the faith with Jesus.

How long has it been since you've shared with your friends what great things the Lord has done for you?

Ellen White writes,

> Many are longing to grow in grace; they pray over the matter, and are surprised that their prayers are not answered. The Master has given them a work to do whereby they shall grow. Of what value is it to pray when there is need of work? The question is, Are they seeking to save souls for whom Christ died? Spiritual growth depends upon giving to others the light that God has given to you. You are to put forth your best thoughts in active labor to do good, and only good, in your family, in your church, and in your neighborhood.
>
> In place of growing anxious with the thought that you are not growing in grace, just do every duty that presents itself, carry the burden of souls on your heart, and by every conceivable means seek to save the lost. Be kind, be courteous, be pitiful; speak in humility of the blessed hope; talk of the love of Jesus; tell of His goodness, His mercy, and His righteousness; and cease to worry as to whether or not you are growing. Plants do not grow through any conscious effort. . . . The plant is not in continual worriment about its growth; it just grows under the supervision of God.
>
> The only way to grow in grace is to be interestedly doing the very work Christ has enjoined upon us to do—interestedly engaged to the very extent of our ability to be helping and blessing those who need the help we can give them.[2]

Notice the clues. Talk of the love of Jesus. Tell of His goodness, His mercy, His righteousness, and don't worry about growing. You see, there is a sequence in this growth process: Bible study, prayer, and witness.

THE SEQUENCE OF GROWTH

You must have something to share before you can share. Right?

You come into court, and you're supposed to be a witness. The judge says, "Who are you?"

"I'm a witness."

"All right."

They swear you in. And the judge says, "You were at the scene?"

"No, sir."

"Were you at the accident? Did you see it?"

"No, I wasn't there."

He says, "Well, then, get out of my courtroom!"

There is a sequence, but you will find that if you begin with Bible study, prayer, and a robust devotional life, it will be meaningful only for a while. If you do not get involved in outreach and serving others, your devotional life will grow sour and stale.

These three things go together, but there is a sequence. You start with your experience with Jesus. Then you have something to share.

In the book *We Thought We Heard the Angels Sing,* Lieutenant James C. Whittaker tells about a plane that went down in the Pacific during World War II. The soldiers were surrounded by water—but they had nothing to drink.

One by one, they got weaker and weaker until they were not much more than a bunch of skeletons out bobbing on the surface of the sea. The sun mercilessly burned them. They buried one man at sea—after they considered eating him.

Now put yourself on that raft. You are on the edge of starvation, weak and emaciated.

Suppose I come along in my speedboat. I ask, "What's wrong with you?"

You stare through sunken eyes, as if trying to grasp a mirage.

Then I start in on my prepared lecture. "What you need is more exercise."

"Rubbish!" you protest. "You need more brains. I don't need exercise, I need more food." Food comes before exercise.

The experience with Christ comes before witness. That's why we have been so weak and insipid in our Christian witness. If we don't eat, we have nothing to say. And when we do have something to say, it will be difficult to keep quiet.

These are the ingredients of growth in grace—the very ingredients that most of us have grossly ignored much of our Christian lives. Stop trying to hang on the clothesline post. You will not grow by trying to grow. You grow by eating, breathing, and exercising.

THE CLASSROOM

FIRST-GRADE ART

By: Claire Haffner 2012

SECOND-GRADE COMPUTERS

At Crosswalk.com, Pastor Adrian Rogers offers the following suggestions on "How to Have a Meaningful Quiet Time:"

- Get still and quiet.
- Get into the Word of God.
- Record what God has given you.

- Now you're ready to pray.
- Begin to share out of your quiet time.
- Finally, obey what God tells you.[3]

THIRD-GRADE BIBLE

"But grow in the grace and knowledge of our Lord and Savior Jesus Christ" (2 Peter 3:18).

"Grow! Grow in grace. Grow in understanding. Grow in Jesus Christ, our Lord and Savior" (2 Peter 3:18, our paraphrase).

FOURTH-GRADE WRITING

An unknown author writes, "Fellowship with God is the privilege of all, and the unceasing experience of but a few."

FIFTH-GRADE MATH

Study + Prayer + Witness = Growth

ENDNOTES

1. Ellen G. White, *The Desire of Ages,* 83.

2. Ellen G. White, *My Life Today* (Washington, DC: Review and Herald®, 1952), 103.

3. Adrian Rogers, "How to Have a Meaningful Quiet Time," Crosswalk, accessed September 2, 2013 http://www.crosswalk.com/devotionals/how-to-have-a-meaningful-quiet-time-1338122.html.

– 10 –

GRAPE EXPECTATIONS

In his classic book *The Life You've Always Wanted,* John Ortberg tells about a cranky, cantankerous old man in his church named Hank. He was ornery and offensive and had been for decades. Hank never changed. Moreover, nobody in the church seemed to expect Hank to change. Ortberg reflects,

> It was as if everyone simply expected that his soul would remain withered and sour year after year, decade after decade. No one seemed bothered by the condition. It was not an anomaly that caused head-scratching bewilderment. No church consultants were called in. No emergency meetings were held to probe the strange case of this person who followed the church's general guidelines for spiritual life and yet was nontransformed.
>
> The church staff did have some expectations. We expected that Hank would affirm certain religious beliefs. We expected that he would attend services, read the Bible, support the church financially, pray regularly, and avoid certain sins. But here's what we didn't expect: *We didn't expect that he would progressively become the way Jesus would be if he were in Hank's place.* We didn't assume that each year would find him a more compassionate, joyful, gracious, winsome personality. We didn't anticipate that he was on the way to becoming a source of delight and courtesy who overflowed with "rivers of living water." So we were not shocked when it didn't happen. We would have been surprised if it did![1]

I think Ortberg is spot on with this summary: "Because . . . we do not expect people to experience ongoing transformation, we are not led to question whether perhaps the standard prescriptions for spiritual growth being given in the church are truly adequate to lead people into a transformed way of life."[2]

In what other discipline would we tolerate such a lack in growth?

Intellectually, we expect people to grow. In school, we are rightfully concerned if a kid does not mature beyond the fifth grade. To have a sixty-year-old man struggling to pass fifth grade after fifty years of trying is problematic, right? Don't you think teachers and school administrators would be very concerned with such a scenario?

Physically speaking, we expect growth. Imagine a patient stuck in the same hospital room for fifty years. Certainly, hospital administrators and health care providers would have some questions. "Is the patient taking his medications?"

"Oh yes. He is compliant with all the treatments and therapies that we have prescribed."

"And he has been in our hospital for five decades?"

"Yep."

In schools and in hospitals, we expect maturation, healing, and growth. But in church, nobody seems too upset by people who fail to mature beyond the juvenile spirituality of a fifth-grader.

The Bible tells us, "The fruit of the Spirit is love, joy, peace, forbearance, kindness, goodness, faithfulness, gentleness and self-control" (Galatians 5:22, 23). So is it really all that crazy to expect Christians to model these virtues? That is, to grow to be more loving, joyful, peaceful, and so on? Then why is it OK for folks to actively participate in the community of faith for decades and never seem to bear much fruit?

Ellen White offers this insight:

> I feel a deep anxiety that the youthful disciples of Christ may grow in grace and in the knowledge of the truth. Progression is as much a law of spiritual as of physical life. The Scriptures speak of our growing up into Christ. Young converts are represented as babes, who need the tender care of those older in experience than themselves. They cannot by one great effort attain to the perfection of Christian growth. They are children, who must advance, little by little, until they reach the stature of men and women in Christ.[3]

WHAT DID JESUS SAY ABOUT PRODUCING FRUIT?

In John 15, Jesus had some pointed words on this topic of growth and fruit bearing. Let's consider the passage.

Jesus said, "I am the true vine, and my Father is the gardener" (John 15:1). Immediately, Jesus would have captured the attention of His listeners for they were well versed in the imagery of vineyards. The vine was the symbol of the nation of Israel. It was the emblem on the coins of the Maccabees. One of the glories of the temple was the great golden vine on the front of the Holy Place. So Jesus used a common picture in that culture.

Jesus continued, "He cuts off every branch in me that bears no fruit, while every branch that does bear fruit he prunes so that it will be even more fruitful" (verse 2).

For her book *Scouting the Divine: My Search for God in Wine, Wool, and Wild Honey*, author Margaret Feinberg traveled to California to hang out with vintners. She wondered, *How do you read John 15, not as a theologian, but in light of what a vintner might do every day?* In other words, what does Jesus' command to abide in the vine mean to a vintner? She discovered that vintners must be very patient. She writes,

> The first year a vintner plants shoots of vines rather than seeds be-cause these yield the strongest vines. At the end of the first growing season, he cuts them back. A second year passes. He cuts them back again. Only after the third year does he see his first viable clusters of grapes. Serious vintners leave those clusters on the vines. For most vintners, it's not until year four that they'll bring in their first harvest.
>
> For those growing grapes for winemaking, they'll bottle their harvest, but won't taste the fruit of their labors until year seven or eight. Most vineyards in Napa Valley won't reach a breakeven point for their investment until year 15, 18, or beyond.[4]

Applying these insights to her spiritual life, Feinberg writes,

> Sometimes I look at my own life and wonder, *Why am I not more fruit-ful? And why does pruning have to hurt so much? Why does cultivating a healthy crop take so long?* Yet those questions circle around the here and now. God's perspective is much different. Like a good vineyard owner, he knows how to bring about fruitfulness better than I ever will. And he is patient with me, more patient than I am with myself.[5]

Perhaps you're discouraged because you have not experienced the kind of growth that you would like in your spiritual journey. Perhaps you know the agony of a self-destructive pattern of behavior, that same old sin that has haunted you for years. In this parable, Jesus says, "Take heart. It's My timetable, not yours. Your job is not to work on bearing more fruit; rather, your job is to abide in Me."

Jesus then said, "You are already clean because of the word I have spoken to you. Remain in me, as I also remain in you. No branch can bear fruit by itself; it must remain in the vine. Neither can you bear fruit unless you remain in me" (verses 3, 4).

"Victorious living and effective soul-winning service are not the product of our better selves and hard endeavours," writes Roy Hession, "but are simply the fruit of the Holy Spirit. We are not called upon to produce the fruit, but simply to bear it."[6] And the only way to "bear" fruit is to abide in Christ. Over and over in this passage, we are told to abide or remain in Jesus. In other words, fruit is the natural result of seeking Jesus day by day.

This is an important distinction. It's not your job to produce the fruits of the Spirit in your life. The truth is—even if you wanted to—you couldn't produce such fruits any more than a leopard could change its spots. You can't produce the fruit of the Spirit, you can only bear the fruit that is the inevitable consequence of a relationship with Jesus.

Jesus then reiterated, "I am the vine; you are the branches. If you remain in me and I in you, you will bear much fruit; apart from me you can do nothing" (verse 5).

Do you remember the 2011 Super Bowl commercial that pictured a child dressed in a Darth Vader costume attempting to use the "force" around the house? With the familiar *Star Wars* music associated with Darth Vader playing in the background, the boy marches down the hallway and then raises his hands dramatically toward a dryer in the utility room. Hocus pocus! Nothing happens.

Next, the young Darth points his hands at the family dog lying on the floor. The dog looks up quizzically, but again nothing happens.

Darth does not give up. Now in the bedroom, he raises his hands forcefully toward a doll seated on the bed. The doll stares back blankly without budging an inch.

One more time, he raises his hands and points them dramatically at the Volkswagen in the driveway. He waits, hands upraised. Suddenly, the car's yellow turn signals light up, and the engine starts!

The startled child stumbles backward. We see that his playful father had started the car from the kitchen using a push-button ignition. The amazed child whirls to look toward the house, and then back again toward the car.

Just as this kid could do nothing without the intervention of the father, so we can do nothing in the work of the Lord apart from God. When spiritual things happen, we can be sure that our Father did it.

"If you do not remain in me," Jesus continued, "you are like a branch that is thrown away and withers; such branches are picked up, thrown into the fire and burned" (verse 6). The wood from the vine was so soft it was considered useless. According to ancient law, God's people were required to bring wood to the temple for the altar fires. But the wood of the vine could not even be used for this purpose. The only thing that could be done with the wood pruned from a vine was to make a bonfire with it and destroy it. So Jesus alludes to this familiar ancient custom.

Then Jesus said, "If you remain in me and my words remain in you, ask whatever you wish, and it will be done for you. This is to my Father's glory, that you bear much fruit, showing yourselves to be my disciples" (verses 7, 8).

TAKE-HOME LESSONS FROM OUR TOUR

Tour a vineyard and you're likely to learn something. Similarly, our tour through this text teaches us about our spiritual journey with God. Of the many take-home lessons that we might highlight from this tour, let me suggest three. Based on Christ's teaching, what can we expect from God in our walk with Him? What are the "grape" expectations for a fruitful and productive journey with Jesus?

1. EXPECT GOD'S PRUNING

First, Jesus makes it clear that there is a pruning process. Notice again verse 2: "Every branch that does bear fruit he prunes so that it will be even more fruitful."

Do you want to be fruitful? There is no other way to grow and produce good works except through pruning.

Vines left unattended will sprawl in every direction and produce huge canopies of shoots, leaves, and branches. But unless that canopy is controlled, the vine will yield minimal fruit.

Pruning is counterintuitive; after all, it seems to be excising the healthiest part of the vine. Although the vine may look healthy, the truth is it's not bearing much fruit. All show and no tell.

Jesus seemed concerned that the disciples might be facing this same problem. Jesus was not interested in showy disciples anymore than He wants to recruit showy Christians in this postmodern world. Jesus wants to see fruit in His followers.

While visiting the vineyards of Napa Valley, Margaret Feinberg came to this same understanding. Listen to her personal reflection:

> The principle of pruning in theory was familiar, but not until that morning in the vineyard did it finally become a pressing desire. I had felt moments of pruning in my past—loss of jobs, relationships, opportunities, and even health—but only in the vineyard did I get a glimpse of the fruitfulness that erupts. The grape bunches that weighed eight to ten pounds came from the vines that had been pruned. The grapes looked like gigantic gifts of life under the green canopy—a portrait of what, deep down inside, I desire in my own life.[7]

Urban Holmes adds this:

> Any good gardener knows that beautiful roses require careful pruning. Pieces of a living plant have to die. It cannot just grow wild. We cannot simply "celebrate growth." It is more than to be regretted, it is tragic that we seem to have lost the insight that growth in Christ requires careful pruning. Pieces of us by our intentional action need to die if we are to become the person that is in God's vision. [The Gardener is] not cutting away a cancerous growth, but making room for intended growth.[8]

Consider the hedge-type plants that guard the kingdom and grace the landscape at Walt Disney World. You'll find bushes that look like every cartoon character from Mickey Mouse to Donald Duck. I know it's the Magic Kingdom and all, but these shapes don't just magically appear. By trimming the bushes regularly, horticulturists shape the plants into the forms they envision.

In a similar fashion, God prunes our lives to shape us into the image of Jesus. This may involve removing sin or other distractions from our lives. At times, God's pruning is painful, but over time, God is changing us to be more like His Son.

In the pruning process, know this: your heavenly Father is never closer to you than when He is pruning you. Sometimes He cuts away the dead wood that might cause trouble; but often He cuts off the living tissue that is robbing you of spiritual vigor. This involves cutting away the good and the better so that we might enjoy the best.

Elizabeth Sherrill reflects on a statement she read in a book on osteoporosis prevention:

> "Like all living tissue, bone is constantly being broken down and reformed." The words seemed to apply not only to our bodies but to the perpetual Christian emphasis on brokenness. . . . [It] was the word *living* that leaped out at me. It's living tissue that is continually torn down and rebuilt. As long as my relationship to God is alive, this biological fact seems to suggest the tearing-down process will be part of it. . . . There can be no growth without pruning, no rebirth without death.[9]

Did you catch that? As long as your relationship with God is active and alive, there will be pruning. That's just the way God rolls. But the end result is what we would choose in the first place if we could see the end from the beginning.

One final observation about pruning: you will never see a branch pruning another branch. The responsibility of pruning and shaping the vines is not that of the other branches. Sometimes in the church, it seems that branches want to fix and clean up and reprimand other branches. Don't get trapped in that. The work of pruning belongs to God and God alone.

2. Expect God's Presence

The second thing we can expect is the presence of God through all of this. In verse 4, the promise is clear: "Remain in me," Jesus said, "and I will remain in you" (NCV). It is possible to live each moment in the presence of God. This is the most life-changing spiritual principle that I know. When you begin to live every second in the awareness of God's presence, you begin to go really deep with God.

The apostle Paul tells us to "pray continually" (1 Thessalonians 5:17). This is obviously not a command to live 24/7 on our knees in the closet. Regardless of your activity, you can remain in Jesus; you can spend every moment in prayer, that is, in continual dialogue with your best Friend.

I learned this lesson as a freshman in high school at Shenandoah Valley Academy in New Market, Virginia. Leaving home for the first time, it was quite intimidating to find my way on a strange new campus of older kids who seemed to have it all together. Suppressing my fears, I signed up during the first quarter for intramural football. As fate would have it, John, the best athlete in the school, selected me. (I was picked last, of course, but I was a part of John's team all the same!)

GRAPE EXPECTATIONS – 113

As it turned out, the first game would be decided by the final play. With three seconds remaining, our team trailed by four points. It was simple: score a touchdown or lose the game.

In the huddle, John called the play. "Let's catch them off guard," he said. "Rather than hiking the ball to me, hike it to, um, to—" He was pointing at me. He had lost my name but called my number. Then he barked my orders. "Listen up, number twelve, here's what you do. Hold the ball for three seconds, then heave down the middle of the field. Don't worry. I'll be there. I'll catch it. I'll score a touchdown, and we will win this game. OK! Break!"

"Huh?" I stood there, quivering on the twenty-yard line. After all, this game mattered. I would be writing about this game thirty years later. This was not some pickup game at a church social. This was intramural, and the whole game was resting on my shaking shoulders!

As the team lined up, I started praying. "Oh, God," I begged, "I need a miracle. If you can part the Red Sea, if you can feed five thousand with a few loaves of bread, if you can raise the dead, *PLEEEEEEAAAAASSSSSSSEEEEEE,* deliver this pigskin into John's hands." I had never faced anything this big before.

When I called the signals, rather than saying something like, "Forty-three, twenty-six, hut, hut," I accidentally yelled exactly what I was thinking. I shouted, "Dear heavenly Father!"

The defense stared, confused. They didn't know if I was trying to be funny or sacrilegious. They froze.

Our center alertly hiked the ball. John raced down the field. I chucked the ball as hard as I could. It wobbled in the air and found John—standing alone in the middle of the field. He caught the ball. He raced to the end zone. We won the game!

We pulled off the greatest victory in the history of intramurals at Shenandoah Valley Academy. The next day, the president invited us to the White House. Then we went to Disney World. Well, OK, the story kind of grows in my own mind.

Here's the deal: whether you're playing football or sitting in traffic or eating Cracker Jacks or texting in church or standing in line at the post office or drifting off to sleep or reprimanding your child or studying for the final, you can seize that moment for prayer. Talk to Jesus. This is how intimacy is nurtured.

Brother Lawrence contends,

> The most holy practice, the nearest to daily life, and the most essential for the spiritual life, is the practice of the presence of God, that is to find joy in His divine company and to make it a habit of life, speaking humbly and conversing lovingly with Him at all times, every moment, without rule or restriction, above all at times of temptation, distress, dryness, and revulsion, and even of faithlessness and sin.[10]

This is what it looks like to remain in Jesus. As you do this, He will remain in you.

3. EXPECT GOD'S POWER

One more expectation: expect God's power. You do not live a productive, fruitful life in your power. You must depend totally on God for the power to live a life of holiness. Notice verse 5: "I am the vine; you are the branches. If you remain in me and I in you, *you will bear much fruit;* apart from me you can do nothing" (verse 5; emphasis added).

In your own willpower, you can do nothing. In God's power, you will bear much fruit. As Lloyd Ogilvie once quipped, "Without God, we can't; without us, He won't."

In 1927, the director Cecil B. DeMille cast British-born actor H. B. Warner as Jesus in his famous silent film *The King of Kings.* Warner, who nineteen years later played the druggist in *It's a Wonderful Life,* was kept on a short leash during the filming of *The King of Kings.* Cecil B. DeMille was concerned that any behavior by the lead actor deemed inconsistent with the image of Christ would result in negative publicity for the film.

Consequently, DeMille enforced strict measures to ensure that Warner kept up a good Jesus image (or what DeMille *thought* would be a good representation of Jesus). Both Warner and his costar, Dorothy Cumming (who played Mary, the mother of Jesus), had to sign agreements that barred them for five years from appearing in film roles that might compromise their "holy" screen images. During the filming, Warner was driven to the set with blinds drawn, covered in a black veil. DeMille separated Warner from the other cast members, even forcing him to eat alone every day. Warner couldn't play cards, go to ballgames, ride in a convertible, or go swimming. To ensure the cast and crew observed a suitable level of reverence toward Warner as Jesus Christ, no one except director Cecil B. DeMille was allowed to talk to him when he was in costume.

Ironically, the strict regimen of rules didn't make Warner more holy. Instead, all of the pressure to be more Christlike without having the power or forgiveness of Jesus seemed to drive Warner over the edge. During the production of *The King of Kings,* rather than act more like Jesus, Warner merely relapsed into his addiction to alcohol. Also, he was involved in a scandal with an anonymous woman who was determined to blackmail Cecil B. DeMille by ruining the production. It is believed that DeMille paid the woman on the condition that she leave the United States.[11]

Apart from God's power, you cannot be holy. Try, try, try. Sign a contract if you like. Collect a big check as motivation to be good. Grit your teeth. Clench your fists. Make your promises. But your best efforts are futile apart from the power of Jesus living in you to produce good works. God says, "You can't force these things. They only come about through my Spirit" (Zechariah 4:6, *The Message*).

In the end, it's all about Jesus. His Spirit abiding in you to produce good works.

THE CLASSROOM

FIRST-GRADE ART

SECOND-GRADE COMPUTERS

Text message from God:
HRU?
MUSM
CTC?
H2CUS
LYLC,
God

For the technologically challenged:
How are you?
Miss you so much!
Care to chat?
Hope to see you soon.
Love you like crazy,
God

Third-Grade Bible

"Live in me. Make your home in me just as I do in you. In the same way that a branch can't bear grapes by itself but only by being joined to the vine, you can't bear fruit unless you are joined with me" (John 15:4, *The Message*).

"Let's live together," Jesus says. "We will enjoy intimate communion. As we do life together, I promise that you will become more loving, more joyful, more peaceful, more patient, more faithful, more self-controlled, gentler, kinder, milder, and altogether better. If we do not do life together, I promise that you will not grow into this kind of a person" (John 15:4, our paraphrase).

Fourth-Grade Writing

Russell Moore writes, "For too long, we've called unbelievers to 'invite Jesus into your life.' Jesus doesn't want to be in your life. Your life's a wreck. Jesus calls you into his life. And his life isn't boring or purposeless or static. It's wild and exhilarating and unpredictable."[12]

Fifth-Grade Math

Fruitfulness = I remain in Christ + Christ remains in me

Endnotes

1. John Ortberg, *The Life You've Always Wanted* (Grand Rapids, MI: Zondervan, 1997), 32; emphasis in the original.

2. Ibid., 33.

3. Ellen G. White, "Christian Growth," *The Youth's Instructor,* December 5, 1883.

4. Margaret Feinberg, "Napa Valley on Leadership," Q: Ideas for the Common Good, accessed July 11, 2013, http://www.qideas.org/essays/napa-valley-on-leadership.aspx?page=3.

5. Ibid.

6. Roy Hession, "The Dove and the Lamb," in *The Calvary Road* (Fort Washington, PA: Christian Literature Crusade, 1955), accessed July 11, 2013 http://www.worldinvisible.com/library/hession/calvary%20road/chapter%205.htm.

7. Feinberg, "Napa Valley on Leadership," http://www.qideas.org/essays/napa-valley-on-leadership.aspx?page=4.

8. Urban T. Holmes III, quoted in Steve Ridenour, "A Good Day to Die," Steve Ridenour, accessed October 23, 2013, http://sridenour52.webs.com/agooddaytodie.htm.

9. Elizabeth Sherrill, *Journey Into Rest* (n.p.: Kingsway Communication, 1991).

10. Brother Lawrence, quoted in "Prayer Minstry," St. Paul Lutheran Church, accessed July 12, 2013, http://splconline.com/ministries/prayer/.

11. "The King of Kings: Trivia," IMDb, accessed July 12, 2013 http://www.imdb.com/title/tt0018054/trivia.

12. Russell Moore, "A Purpose-Driven Cosmos," *Christianity Today,* February 2012, 31.

– 11 –

USING YOUR WILL

One day I was driving with a friend in my speedboat. We were skimming along at a hundred miles an hour, barely touching the water. But for some reason, I got the impression that we weren't getting anywhere.

So I took an oar and tried to row. The oar slipped off into the water. "Well," I said, "I think I wasn't holding tight enough to the oar."

So I took out the other oar and held on real tight, trying to row again. Guess what happened to both the oar and me!

That was a parable.

Ever been traveling across the United States on a jumbo jet and decide that you're not getting there fast enough, so you open the door and decide to help things along?

While I can't speak to his motives, that's what Alexander Herrera attempted on May 27, 2013, on Alaska Airlines Flight 132 from Anchorage to Portland. After mumbling some unusual statements, he bolted toward the emergency exit. Passengers jumped into action, restraining him using shoelaces and seat-belt extensions. Upon landing, he was immediately arrested by FBI agents at Portland International Airport on a charge of interfering with a flight crew. He was booked into the Multnomah County Detention Center.

The lesson? It's not smart to open a plane door and help things along. The plane is plenty capable of flying without your efforts.

SANCTIFICATION BY FAITH ALONE?

So when it comes to sanctification, is it God's doing entirely or do we need to stick our oar in the water or poke an arm out the airplane window to help things move along? Are we transformed by faith plus effort? And if sanctification happens by faith alone, then what role does our will play?

The apostle Paul helps to answer these questions. Notice his desire for God's people: "May God himself, the God of peace, sanctify you through and through. May your whole spirit, soul and body be kept blameless at the coming of our Lord Jesus Christ. The one who calls you is faithful, and he will do it" (1 Thessalonians 5:23, 24).

So are we supposed to do anything as God sanctifies us "through and through"? Yes. We are supposed to let Him do it. And the way we let Him do it is through surrender.

We come under His control by our own choice, and this control will be maintained by the continual relationship day by day. That's all we can do. But it's the greatest battle that you will ever fight. And it is a legitimate battle for you to engage in. You are to be very active toward that.

In this daily, ongoing relationship, you are invited to be passive toward fighting the enemy and the battle where the battle isn't. Most of us have been fighting the battle where the battle isn't instead of fighting the battle where the battle is.

In Romans 7:18, Paul describes the frustration of a Christian who hasn't discovered sanctification by faith alone: "For I know that in me (that is, in my flesh,) dwelleth no good thing: for to will is present with me; but how to perform that which is good I find not" (KJV). Can you relate to his struggle?

Suppose I advertise that I am going to put on a concert and present some of the songs of the masters. Now that's not a bad idea; people like to hear great singing. And I believe myself to be a great singer. So the advertisements go out, and you come to my concert.

I have willed to do a good thing.

You, along with thousands of other music lovers, arrive. The curtain rises. I stand in the center of the stage. The pianist plays the introduction. I open my mouth. The auditorium empties.

I have the desire to do what is good, but I cannot carry it out. I have the will but lack the tools.

WILL VERSUS WILLPOWER

To grasp this concept, it is important to differentiate between will and willpower. If you study the definition of *will,* it has to do with the power of choice. To will is to choose.

Now, usually we use the term *willpower* in a different sense. We say willpower is equated with backbone, self-discipline, grit, and determination. We say, "That's my problem: I have a backbone like wet spaghetti, and I lack the self-discipline required to be good."

So let's say that the will is the power to choose, and willpower is the self-discipline and grit to get things done. Substituting these new definitions into the text then renders Paul's words in this way: "For to *choose* is present with me; but how to *perform* that which is good I find not." Have you ever chosen to do the right thing only to find yourself utterly lacking in willpower when it comes to following through on your good intentions? Your willpower is too anemic to carry out your will.

Another text from Paul that makes this distinction between will and willpower is Philippians 2:12, 13: "Therefore, my dear friends, . . . continue to work out your salvation with fear and trembling, for it is God who works in you to will and to act in order to fulfill his good purpose."

Legalists love to quote that command to "work out your salvation with fear and trembling." "See there," they gloat, "you gotta work at it. Work hard. If you don't feel like doing it, then grit your teeth and get a little discipline in your life and do it anyway. God wants to see a little trembling!"

Using this distinction between will and willpower, however, let's reconsider Paul's punch line. Here is a paraphrase of verse 13: "It is God who works in you to supply the power to surrender your freedom of choice and give you all the self-discipline and grit you need in order to fulfill His good purpose."

Ellen White provides helpful insight. In *Steps to Christ,* she writes,

> Many are inquiring, "How am I to make the surrender of myself to God?" You desire to give yourself to Him, but you are weak in moral power, in slavery to doubt, and controlled by the habits of your life of sin. Your promises and resolutions are like ropes of sand. You cannot control your thoughts, your impulses, your affections. The knowledge of your broken promises and forfeited pledges weakens your confidence in your own sincerity, and causes you to feel that God cannot accept you; but you need not despair. What you need to understand is the true force of the will.[1]

Wow! Can I ever relate? "Weak in moral power"? Yes. "Slavery to doubt"? Check. "Controlled by the habits of your life of sin"? Absolutely. "Resolutions are like ropes of sand"? Guilty. "You cannot control your thoughts, your impulses, your affections"? Yep. That's me.

Next, she says that we need not despair. Rather, we need to understand the true force of the will. A quick glance prompts me to say, "Yes! That's my problem. I need more force to my will!"

So I try to develop more force to my will. You know—force myself to do things that I don't want to do. Force myself to drink sixteen glasses of water without stopping. Force myself to stay out of the cookie jar. Force myself to stop blowing up at my kids. After all, I'm developing more will, right?

But I've failed to read on where she explains the will. What is the will? Listen to her answer: "[The will] is the governing power in the nature of man, the power of decision, or of choice."[2]

"Well," I reason, "if the will is the power of choice, then I am going to personalize this and wherever it says *will,* I'll substitute *power of choice.*" Doing this proves enlightening.

"What you need to understand is the true force of the *power of choice.* . . . Everything depends on the right action of the *power of choice.* The *power of choice* God has given to me; it is mine to exercise. You cannot change your heart, you cannot of yourself give to God its affections; but you can *choose* to serve Him."

Notice she isn't saying you can choose what to do. She is saying you can choose whom to serve. Jesus made it clear, "No one can serve two masters" (Luke 16:13). You will be controlled by one of two powers. You can choose to place yourself under the control of God or Satan. *There is no middle ground!* Placing yourself under the control of God brings freedom, because it is the control of love and love brings freedom. The control of Satan is puppetry, because there is not love; it is nothing but force and duress. You will serve one master or the other.

Now what does that word *serve* suggest? It means becoming a servant. I can choose to become His servant; therefore, I choose to let Him become my Master. And the Master is in control.

What this means, then, is that you can give Him your will, that is, your power of choice.

Hold on! I can give Him my power of choice? I thought that the power of choice was the thing that made me uniquely created in the image of God. You mean the surrender of my will is the surrender of my power of choice?

Yes.

God will then work in you to will and to do according to His pleasure. Thus, your whole nature will be brought under the control of the Spirit of Christ. Your actions will be centered upon Him; your thoughts will be in harmony with His thoughts.

Through the right exercise of the power of choice, an interior change may be made in your life. By yielding up your power of choice to Christ, you ally yourself with the power that is above all principalities and powers. You will then have strength from above to hold you steadfast. And thus, through continuing surrender, constantly yielding your power of choice to Him, you will be empowered to live a new life—the life of faith.

Every person is free to choose what power will control his or her life. In this way, our power of choice is never compromised. We never surrender our power of choice as to who will rule over us. By steadfastly keeping your will (that is, your power of choice) on the Lord's side, every temptation will be brought into captivity by the will of Jesus.

SPIRITUAL FORMATION? HYPNOTISM?

The only thing that we can do with our will is to choose which power is going to rule over us and control us. "But," you argue, "isn't that hypnotism? Isn't that dancing dangerously close to the perils of spiritual formation and the emptying of one's mind? Isn't it dangerous to yield your mind to another power other than your own?"

You may cite *The Ministry of Healing* where Ellen White has some pointed words about this: "It is not God's purpose that any human being should yield his mind and will to the control of another. . . . He is not to look to any human being. . . . In the dignity of his God-given manhood [and womanhood] he is to be controlled by God Himself."[3]

Note that it is possible then to be controlled by God Himself and still preserve the dignity of my God-given personhood. Can you trust God that this is possible?

Why is God opposed to hypnotism? Because it is man playing God. It is man, or the devil, taking the prerogative that belongs to God alone as our Creator. God invites us as His created beings to come under the control of Him only and under no one else. This is a part of His entire plan of salvation and restoration.

Now consider the statement in a different light by reversing it. "It is God's purpose that every human being should yield his mind and will to the control of God." This is God's purpose.

Consider also this statement: "God does not control our minds without our consent."[4] Now reverse it. "God does control our minds with our consent."

Are you willing?

Nick Vujicic provides a picture of surrender. In 1982, he was born with tetra-amelia syndrome, a rare genetic disorder. Nick has no arms or legs, although he has two small feet attached to his torso. As a child, Nick struggled emotionally and physically to accept his condition. But today, as a follower of Christ, he says that he enjoys "a ridiculously good life." He writes,

> When I'm asked how I can claim a ridiculously good life when I have no arms or legs, [people] assume I'm suffering from what I lack. They inspect my body and wonder how I could possibly give my life to God, who allowed me to be born without limbs. Others have attempted to soothe me by saying that God has all the answers and then when I'm in heaven I will find out his intentions. Instead, I choose to believe and live by what the Bible says, which is that God is the answer today, yesterday, and always.
>
> When people read about my life or witness me living it, they are prone to congratulate me for being victorious over my disabilities. I tell them that my victory came in surrender. It comes every day when I acknowledge that I can't do this on my own, so I say to God, "I give it to You!" Once I yielded, the Lord took my pain and turned it into something good. . . .
> . . . He gave my life meaning when no one and nothing else could provide it.[5]

> If God can take someone like me, someone without arms and legs, and use me as His hands and feet, He can use anybody. It's not about ability. The only thing God needs from you is a willing heart.[6]

Again, I ask you: Are you willing?

THE CLASSROOM

FIRST-GRADE ART

SECOND-GRADE COMPUTERS

Recently, I received Nick Vujicic's book *Limitless* as a gift for giving a Week of Prayer at a high school in Nick's home country of Australia. Before reading it, I jumped on one of my favorite Web sites, www .goodreads.com to check the reviews. While I had not heard of Nick before, it turns out that lots of people have!

One of the many positive reviews comes from "Create With Joy": "What would your life look like if you truly believed 'with God, all things are possible'? Would your life be radically different if you had the faith of a mustard seed? I think that if we all truly lived with those convictions, our lives might look a lot like Nick Vujicic's."

THIRD-GRADE BIBLE

"For God is working in you, giving you the desire and the power to do what pleases him" (Philippians 2:13, NLT).

"OK, let's get real: it's not you working real hard to make yourself all pretty and perfect, it's God. *All God.* Only He can change you from the heart—planting in you the desire to do what pleases Him. And not to worry, He'll supply the power as well" (our paraphrase).

FOURTH-GRADE WRITING

Dwight L. Moody said, "Spread out your petition before God, and then say, 'Thy will, not mine, be done.' The sweetest lesson I have learned in God's school is to let the Lord choose for me."

FIFTH-GRADE MATH

Sanctification = Faith + 0

ENDNOTES

1. Ellen G. White, *Steps to Christ,* 47.

2. Ibid.

3. Ellen G. White, *The Ministry of Healing* (Mountain View, CA: Pacific Press®, 1942), 242.

4. Ellen G. White, *The Desire of Ages,* 258.

5. Nick Vujicic, *Limitless* (Colorado Springs, CO: WaterBrook, 2013), 147, 148.

6. Ibid., 2.

– 12 –

VICTORY BY GRACE—
OR GIMMICKS?

When talking about righteousness by faith alone, inevitably questions arise. "All right," people have said to me, "we understand we are not supposed to work on our sins. We are supposed to put more of our attention and our direction toward a relationship with Jesus. But in the mean time, what do we do with our sins? And suppose it takes us a while to come into this relationship with Jesus? Aren't you afraid that if a person stops focusing on trying to do what's right in order to begin to know Jesus that there might be an interim of anarchy?"

School administrators—particularly in boarding academies—express grave fears about this. They get nervous when I say that I would like to see our young people stop trying so hard to do what's right and start training to know Jesus as a personal Friend and that if they did, it just might be surprising what Jesus is then able to do in their lives.

Others object that some people will stop trying to do what is right now in order to learn to know Jesus later, and thus open the door for a season of mayhem. I propose that this is an unfounded fear because of the obvious conclusion.

The strong person, who has succeeded in behaving morally through his will-power and backbone, without Christ, is going to continue doing what's right for selfish reasons—whether he accepts salvation through faith in Christ or not. A person who has succeeded in staying out of trouble and out of jail will not suddenly scrap everything that kept him out of trouble and out of jail.

I haven't yet seen a person who became immoral and went to jail because he decided that righteousness by faith meant that he could go ahead and do whatever he had always wanted to do anyway, so that grace might abound.

There are too many worldly benefits to staying out of trouble; if you have succeeded so far in externally controlling your life and your actions, I dare say that in the interim you are going to continue succeeding externally whether or not you are into salvation through faith in Jesus alone.

I'd also argue that the weak person who hasn't succeeded in doing right outwardly is going to continue not succeeding and that he won't be any worse off than he was before. The only one who fears that righteousness by faith will promote license is the one who has some kind of false belief that a weak person could do better if only he would try harder. But that's a false hope. Is the strong person fearful that another strong person might stop trying to do good and become immoral?

Someone suggested to me that the real problem could be this: "Realizing that the weak person might find an excuse or reason to continue being weak, the strong person becomes jealous, because she has always been weak herself inside and wishes she could be weak outwardly, too, just for the fun of it." Is it possible that she objects to license for the weak because she wants license for herself?

The elder brother in the story of the prodigal son comes to mind. He's the one who claims his kid brother squandered their dad's money on prostitutes. Nowhere else in the story do you get that salacious detail. Why does the strong-willed older brother bring it up? Perhaps he was jealous because that's how he would have sinned. Maybe he objected to his younger brother's behavior because he wanted license for himself. The father, you will recall, never mentioned the prostitutes or any behavior. He just rejoiced because the kid was home. Moreover, the father explained to the elder brother that if staying at home with Dad was not enough to satisfy his wants then nothing else—not the prostitutes or the parties or the barns or the tractors—would bring contentment.

Here we note a grave misunderstanding of the genuine relationship of faith. The only thing that will keep a husband and wife true to each other is a genuine relationship of love. That relationship is its own biggest safeguard against license.

There is a cheap brand of righteousness by faith. It's the kind in which people don't study God's Word and they don't spend time in prayer and they are not seeking the relationship. They have no devotional life, but they have accepted the motto, the banner, of righteousness by faith as a sort of fad movement. It's a rebellion against legalism, but it's not a beholding of genuine faith.

The big divider between cheap righteousness by faith and the real deal is the devotional life. Without a meaningful, continuing daily devotional life, a person will invariably drag down God's grace to a paltry level of performance rather than a personal friendship, focusing on the fight of sin rather than the fight of faith. Genuine grace is always anchored in the practice of beholding Jesus, partaking of His Word, and continuing a daily experience with Him. Thus, growth in the Christian life is growth in the constancy of full surrender, that is, trusting all the time.

PARTIAL SURRENDER?

It could be argued that there is no such thing as partial surrender. Surrender is either all or nothing.

Think about World War II: Victory in Europe Day, Victory over Japan Day—when victory came to Europe and Asia. What happened? The enemy surrendered.

Did they say, "We surrender all of our machine guns; come on over and get them"?

We likely would have replied, "You're just trying to trick us. You still have submarines and mortars and tanks and planes."

Did they say, "We surrender all of our submarines"?

"No, thanks." They still possessed machine guns and bombs.

When they surrendered, they said, "We surrender ourselves." When they gave up themselves, we didn't have to go over and collect the submarines and the bombs and the machine guns. The surrender of themselves took care of the surrender of the things.

What do we do in the Christian life? We say we will give up our rap CDs. We surrender our novels. We resolve to no longer visit pornographic Web sites. We promise to tame the temper. I have even seen people come down the aisle and burn their sins at the front of the church while teary friends sing "Kumbaya, my Lord, kumbaya." Get the sins all burned up.

We have all kinds of gimmicks, with one common denominator: they are working on the sins—the tanks, the machine guns, and the submarines. When we surrender ourselves, then Jesus takes over the novels, the music, and the temper. We must be vigilant in the fight of faith, not the fight of sin.

It's fascinating and frustrating to realize that because of the behaviorist idea of surrender it is possible for the strong person to give up all kinds of bad habits. Thus, he feels no need for God's grace. You see, I can fool myself into thinking that because I gave up my smoking, drinking, and dancing, I have surrendered and I don't need God. I'm doing just fine, thank you. But wouldn't it be tragic if we ever give the impression that the primary purpose for Christians in the world is to get people to stop smoking, drinking, and dancing? Surrender *must* embrace more than overcoming bad behaviors.

SURRENDER OF CONTROL

There are two important dynamics in play in this conversation about righteousness by faith. First, there is the relationship with Jesus. Second, there is the complete dependence on Him. Both represent a surrender of control.

To revisit an earlier parable, letting Jesus into the car represents that growing friendship. The second step is letting Him stay in the driver's seat; this represents total dependence on Him. So even if we are on-again and off-again, relative to Him doing all the driving, our assurance of salvation is never in question so long as we keep Him in the car. Our dependence upon Him to do all the driving matures as the daily relationship continues.

Another way to think about this is to imagine that you're riding in an elevator. In Christ, you are going upward, to heaven. There will be times when you fall; but so long as you're in the elevator, you're still headed in the right direction. Remember that the next time you fall. As long as you are in Christ, you're still heading to heaven.

How, then, do works fit into the equation? Consider this legend of when the Golden Gate Bridge was constructed: initially, there was no safety net constructed under the bridge. During the first phase of construction, twenty-three men fell to their deaths. Finally, some bright engineer suggested that they suspend a net beneath the bridge. For the modest price of only one hundred thousand dollars, the net was installed.

During the second half of the construction, ten men fell. All of them were saved in the net. But what's amazing is that production increased 25 percent after the net was installed! Why? Because once people knew that they could work—and even fall—without the fear of death, they were more productive. They did better work.

You see, your heavenly Father and Friend does not want you to live with the fear of falling. He wants you to know that there is a net in the shape of a cross anchored beneath you, securing you in your salvation. And in that assurance, you can do better work. The focus of this "work" is letting Him drive the car, surrendering the steering wheel to His control.

Consider a child who joins a family, whether by birth or by adoption. Who is now in control? The parents. Does that mean that the child is never going to fall, that he will never get muddy or soil his diapers? No. But the parents are still in control, and they will stay in control until that child reaches maturity.

My brother and I got jobs one summer. They were our first jobs. We were supposed to scrape trays out in the drying fields. The workers cut fruit in half and put it on the trays in the sun to dry—apricots, peaches, and so on.

We were getting seventy-five cents an hour; we could hardly believe the fabulous amount of money. One day we were hosing the trays. It was hot. All of a sudden, one of us (I am quite certain it was my brother) raised the hose a little too high and got the other guy wet. (No, I think I raised the hose *accidentally* too high; he raised his on purpose.) Soon we were involved in a good old-fashioned water fight.

Our boss, Jim, saw us from a distance. He came running over to tell us that he did not pay us seventy-five cents an hour to do that. We were working for him, we were his servants; he was our boss; he was in control; he was in charge. We goofed.

We were afraid of Jim. He could be an intimidating dude.

A few weeks later, we were picking tomatoes. When you are picking tomatoes and it is almost noon, there is only one thing to do: pick one, eat one. Our boss, Jim, saw us from the window of the kitchen. He came running with three saltshakers—one for my brother, one for me, and one for him.

There is nothing like a fresh tomato right off the vine with some salt. Our boss became our buddy. We began to love him.

He was in charge. Even though we made mistakes on the job, he was still in charge. He was in control, and gradually we learned to follow and to obey because we loved him more and more.

If you become involved in an ongoing relationship with Jesus, this allows Him to be the Administrator of your life. You will swing back and forth. You will fall.

You will fail. But if you continue the relationship, He is the Programmer in charge of the computer. He is your Administrator, and He will continue to lead you and guide you and finish the work that He started in your life.

If you do not have an ongoing relationship with Jesus, this allows the enemy to be the administrator of your life. He may be frustrated by some of the built-in inhibitions that you've carried over from childhood and by the training and background that you have had. There will be times when he will apparently lose, and there might even be times when you look toward heaven when trouble comes. But if you do not have an ongoing relationship with Jesus, the devil is the administrator, and he will take you down.

But if we stay within God's control by choosing an ongoing relationship with Him, He will gradually teach us how to allow Him to be not only the Administrator of our lives but be in actual moment-by-moment control of the steering wheel. He's in charge even, or should I say *especially*, when we are tempted.

TACKLING TEMPTATION

Hebrews 4:14–16 provides this helpful insight on the topic of temptation: "Seeing then that we have a great High Priest who has passed through the heavens, Jesus the Son of God, let us hold fast our confession. For we do not have a High Priest who cannot sympathize with our weaknesses, but was in all points tempted as we are, yet without sin. Let us therefore come boldly to the throne of grace, that we may obtain mercy and find grace to help in time of need" (NKJV).

The translation of verse 15 can be somewhat deceiving. In the Greek, the word *points* is not there. It literally reads, "[Our High Priest] was in all tempted as we are, yet without sin."

Including the word *points* implies that unless Jesus was tempted to watch pornography on the Internet or smoke pot or stuff Himself at Kimble's Ice Cream Parlor, He could not be our High Priest. The issue in sin is not "points," as in specific, naughty behaviors; the issue is relational—dependence versus independence. And Jesus was in all tempted like as we are, to every extent, yet without sin.

In verse 16, we find the key to the issue of temptation: "Let us therefore come boldly to the throne of grace, that we may obtain mercy and find grace to help in time of need" (NKJV). It's straightforward. It's not gimmicky. We can come to God, and then when the temptations hit, we are empowered by God's grace to overcome.

Have you ever tried to overcome temptation with gimmicks? I've tried all of them. Someone told me the way to meet temptation is to quote Scripture. I tried quoting Scripture when temptation came, and it didn't work! Then someone said that when temptation comes, you should sing songs. I tried singing songs—all eleven stanzas. Epic failure! Someone else said to meet temptation with prayer. I tried it. It didn't work. And then I discovered to my chagrin that there were some temptations that I was afraid to meet with prayer—because I was afraid it might work! So I didn't pray!

5—A.Y.M.S.T.F.G.

It's not about gimmicks. It's all about grace.

If we were to read Hebrews 4:16 the way we usually operate, it might read like this: "Let us therefore come boldly to the throne of grace *in time of need* that we may obtain mercy, and find grace to help."

If you are not already in a relationship with Jesus and dependent upon Him *before* temptation comes, you are not going to enjoy a deep, intimate friendship with Him suddenly in your time of need. In other words, if you don't have money in the bank, don't write the check; it's going to bounce. The secret to victory over temptation is to come before the throne of grace long before the temptation ever arrives and to know that close relationship and the constant dependence upon Jesus all the time.

Every genuine victory over every temptation is always won long before the temptation comes. If you presume victory over temptation based on something you do in terms of songs, verses, or prayers, it's not going to work at the time of temptation. And if you trick yourself into thinking it did work, because you are a strong-willed person with lots of backbone, it was only external.

24/7 DEPENDENCE

Authentic victory over temptation is an internal reality. It flows out of a moment-by-moment dependence upon Jesus. In the beginning, a Christian may know that total dependence one hour out of twenty-four. During that one hour, she has absolute, ultimate, and total victory. The devil cannot touch her except to try and separate her from her stance of dependence upon Jesus.

For the growing Christian, the constancy of that surrendered stance is the key. Depending *only* upon Jesus more and more constantly, until the result is someone like Moses who was sanctified to the point that he almost saw the face of God. He was 120 years old. Let's say that just before he died, he was depending totally upon Jesus twenty-three out of twenty-four hours every day.

During those twenty-three hours each day, he has absolute victory over sin. He enjoys the strength of the power of God. But during that one hour when he still depends on himself, he can fail. Did he? Yes, shortly before he died. Why? Read the story, and you'll discover that Moses had become distracted with his enemies and had neglected to keep his sight and his attention on Jesus.

What does that tell you? If Moses—one of the greatest men who ever lived—could fail, don't you ever judge whether or not you are a Christian by your performance or behavior. If Moses had tried to decide whether or not he was a Christian simply by his performance or behavior, he would have been one discouraged man after 120 years, right? Don't do it.

Leave your performance and your behavior up to God, and thank Him for grace in your time of need, whether it is the crisis of temptation or the need for forgiveness. Rest in the good news that we have a great High Priest who knows what it means to struggle with all of the forces of darkness that get unleashed against every human being in an effort to separate us from God. Stay connected to Christ and rely fully upon His work. Surrender your power of choice to Him and trust in His victory.

A COMPLETED WORK

My father believed in work. Every summer, we planted a big garden at my grandpa's house in Attleboro, Massachusetts. The summers could be stifling. It was an endless stream of humidity and weeds and gnats that buzz in your ear when it's a hundred degrees. When my brothers and I were sent to the field to weed the tomatoes, we would cite the man in the parable: "An enemy hath done this" (Matthew 13:28, KJV).

Now I have children of my own. There have been times when it has been a real pleasure to get even with my dad and send my girls out to pull weeds!

But I remember when Dad would join us in that garden. And could he ever pull weeds! For every weed I threw in the wheelbarrow, Dad matched it with a dozen of his own. I would keep working as though I was really working, but I would keep saying under my breath, "Go, Dad, go, go, go! Pull them weeds!"

Now transfer the scene to a heavenly country. One day our great High Priest looks down, and He sees this weed patch of a world. He sees us down here trying, sweating, struggling to pull weeds, and His heart of compassion is stirred. His great heart of love bleeds for His children. So He says, "I will go down, and I will pull the weeds for them." So He comes on a long, expensive trip to demonstrate the concern and compassion of heaven for poor sinners in this world of weeds.

And can Jesus ever pull weeds!

When I realize that He was in all tempted like I am—He knows the separation; He knows the weeds—I say, "How can I help but love that kind of Man?"

THE CLASSROOM

FIRST-GRADE ART

"I am confident that the Creator, who has begun such a great work among you, will not stop in mid-design but will keep perfecting you until the day Jesus the Anointed, our Liberating King, returns to redeem the world" (Philippians 1:6, *The Voice*).

SECOND-GRADE COMPUTERS

Wikipedia, the online encyclopedia, explains *temptation* like this: "Temptation is the desire to perform an action that one may enjoy immediately or in the short term but will probably later regret for various reasons: legal, social, psychological (including feeling guilt), health-related, economic, etc. In the context of religion, temptation is the inclination to sin."

THIRD-GRADE BIBLE

"So let us come boldly to the throne of our gracious God. There we will receive his mercy, and we will find grace to help us when we need it most" (Hebrews 4:16, NLT).

"You don't need to be tentative when it comes to temptation. You go to God. Live in His presence. Trust Him. And you will find grace when you are at your lowest" (Hebrews 4:16, our paraphrase).

FOURTH-GRADE WRITING

Sun Tzu, writing in the late sixth-century B.C., said, "Every battle is won or lost before it is fought."

FIFTH-GRADE MATH

24/7/365 = The goal in trusting Jesus in every temptation

- 13 -

THE WHOLE SHEBANG IN THREE WORDS

"Did you know today is National Declutter Day?" my brother called to tell me more than to ask.

"Really? There is such a day?"

"Oh yes!" he exclaimed. "We have already taken three pickup loads to Goodwill. We hope to dump off two more loads."

By the end of the conversation, I was green with envy. That's when I remembered buying a book entitled *Organize Yourself!* by Ronni Eisenberg. I knew it was somewhere in the garage, but I couldn't find it in the midst of all the clutter.

The only thing I remember about that book is the paragraph I read in the store before purchasing it. The author suggests the best way to get rid of clutter is to pack all the junk you're not using anymore and mark the boxes with the date. Two years from that date, chuck the box without opening it. The theory goes, if you don't miss the stuff in two years, you don't need it.

I thought that was a good idea. I mentioned it to my wife. Woke up the next morning and she had written the date—on my forehead!

Purging clutter is a great thing, wouldn't you agree? This is true in a theological sense as well. With all of our talk about justification, sanctification, righteousness by faith, and so on, it's time to simplify by sharing the gospel in three words.

GUILT

We begin with the word *guilt*. The Bible says, "All have sinned and fall short of the glory of God" (Romans 3:23). Until you understand and accept the fact that we are all guilty, you cannot experience grace.

Even saints struggle with sin. Mind you, we are not always up front about this—especially preachers. We're masters at posturing ourselves as the squeakiest of the clean. Listen carefully, and you'll notice how often pastors tell stories that put themselves in the best possible light.

For example, ever hear a preacher reference a TV show by saying, "I was just flipping through the channels the other day, and I happened to see . . ."? The disclaimer is subtle but meant to be noticed. The preacher hopes you get this message: "I don't watch much TV. I just so happened to have twenty-six seconds between seven Bible studies and thirteen baptisms when I glimpsed a show."

Well, the truth (about this preacher, anyway) is that sometimes I sit down and watch TV. Bag of Cheetos in the left hand, bowl of Ben and Jerry's Chunky Monkey in the right—and I'm not flipping channels. Nor am I watching 3ABN; sometimes I camp on FOX.

As recently as last night, I was flipping through the channels (really!) and heard a TV preacher tell a story of eating pizza with his son. He began by qualifying the story: "I haven't had pizza in two years; but to be with my boy, I compromised my health standards and . . ."

Why the need to explain how long it had been since the last slice of pleasure? Like many Christians, he wanted to preserve an appearance of perfection. But, of course, we know it's all bunkum. If sin is about separating ourselves from God, failing to surrender our power to choose, and jumping into the driver's seat, then "pobody's nerfect." Moreover, the Bible says the consequence of sin is death. In other words, we're all hosed because we're all guilty.

One time I was stopped by a state patrol officer. I was in a big hurry. The officer? Not so rushed. He ambled out of his car and leaned into mine and said, "Do you know why I pulled you over?"

Now, the week before I had seen Jim Carrey's movie *Liar, Liar*. When the officer asked me that question, I couldn't shake from my mind the scene in the movie when Carrey was pulled over and the cop asked him that same question: "Do you know why I pulled you over?"

Because Carrey cannot tell a lie, he answers, "It depends on how long you've been following me."

"Well," scoffs the cop, "why don't you tell me?"

Then Carrey goes through the whole litany, "I ran through a red light, went through a stop sign, rolled through a crosswalk, I was speeding, weaving from one lane to another one, tailgating, almost killed a pedestrian, because I didn't yield a right-of-way."

"Anything else?" the officer asks.

"Yeah, unpaid parking tickets." He opens the glove compartment, and a stack of unpaid parking tickets come cascading out.

Since no other answer came to mind, I just went the confession route. I said, "Look officer, I'm late to a meeting. Whatever the reason you pulled me over, I'm sure I'm guilty. Guilty, guilty, guilty!"

"Interesting," he quipped. "I haven't even told you why I pulled you over. I haven't even given you any explanation. And yet you insist you're guilty. Guilty of what?"

"Well, here's the deal," I backpedaled. "I'm a pastor, so I'm thinking theologically. I'm guilty; you're guilty; we're all guilty, right?"

The policeman wasn't impressed with my theology. Judgment came my way.

Life magazine featured a story in which different people from various walks of life were asked to describe their prayer lives. A prostitute said this: "A lot of people think prostitutes don't have any morals, any religion. But I do. I don't steal. I don't lie. The way I look at it, I'm not sinning. He's not going to judge me. I don't think God judges anybody."

That's where this woman is dead wrong. God will judge each one of us. And on that day, we will all be found wanting—prostitutes and preachers alike. We will all stand guilty and deserving of death before our Judge.

Michael Shermer, publisher of *Skeptic* magazine and author of *The Science of Good and Evil,* writes, "I once had the opportunity to ask Thomas Keneally, author of *Schindler's List,* what he thought was the difference between Oskar Schindler, rescuer of Jews and hero of his story, and Amon Goeth, the Nazi commandant of the Plaszow concentration camp. His answer was revealing. 'Not much,' he said."

Shermer goes on to quote Russian writer Aleksandr Solzhenitsyn: "If only there were evil people somewhere insidiously committing evil deeds, and it were necessary only to separate them from the rest of us and destroy them. But the line dividing good and evil cuts through the heart of every human being. And who is willing to destroy a piece of his own heart?"[1]

When it comes to righteousness, there's no difference between the serial killer and the saint. We all stand guilty before our Holy God. That's the bad news. The good news rings out from Colossians 2:13–15 where we find our second word.

GRACE

The apostle Paul writes,

> When you were dead in your sins and in the uncircumcision of your flesh, God made you alive with Christ. He forgave us all our sins, having canceled the charge of our legal indebtedness, which stood against us and condemned us; he has taken it away, nailing it to the cross. And having disarmed the powers and authorities, he made a public spectacle of them, triumphing over them by the cross.

Here we read the unfathomable good news of God's grace. When we present our list of sins to God, He nails it to the cross and spills His blood over our guilt. There is an exchange—my list for His life, my guilt for His grace, my sinfulness for His sinlessness.

Ellen White explains, "Christ was treated as we deserve, that we might be treated as He deserves. He was condemned for our sins, in which He had no share, that we might be justified by His righteousness, in which we had no share. He suffered the death which was ours, that we might receive the life which was

His. 'With His stripes we are healed.' "[2]

In 1863, during the Civil War, General Thomas "Stonewall" Jackson was accidentally shot by his own troops. His body was laid in the Confederate Capitol in Richmond, Virginia, for two days before his funeral at his home Presbyterian church in Lexington. Tens of thousands of mourning Confederates crowded into the capitol building to look on their beloved leader for the last time.

As the sun was setting on the last day of viewing, the marshal gave orders for the great doors of the Senate chamber to be closed. Just before the gates were finally shut, a rough-looking Confederate soldier in a tattered gray uniform pushed his way forward, tears running down his bearded cheeks.

The marshal in charge was about to turn this insistent man away, when suddenly the soldier lifted up the stump of his right arm and cried out, "By this right arm, which I gave for my country, I demand the right of seeing my general one more time!" The governor of the Commonwealth of Virginia happened to be standing nearby and ordered the marshal to let the soldier in. He said, "He has won entrance by his wounds."

Similarly, we will gain entrance into heaven because of the Cross. We have won entrance by His wounds. "With His stripes we are healed" (Isaiah 53:5, KJV).

That's the gospel: *guilt, grace,* but there is a third word—*growth.*

GROWTH

When the reality of the gospel takes hold of one's heart, it changes a person to the core of his or her being. Having received grace, we are compelled, then, to disperse grace. Listen to how the apostle Paul goes on in this passage in Colossians to spur us on to be transformed into the likeness of Jesus:

> Since, then, you have been raised with Christ, set your hearts on things above, where Christ is, seated at the right hand of God. Set your minds on things above, not on earthly things. For you died, and your life is now hidden with Christ in God. When Christ, who is your life, appears, then you also will appear with him in glory.
>
> Put to death, therefore, whatever belongs to your earthly nature: sexual immorality, impurity, lust, evil desires and greed, which is idolatry. Because of these, the wrath of God is coming. You used to walk in these ways, in the life you once lived. But now you must also rid yourselves of all such things as these: anger, rage, malice, slander, and filthy language from your lips. . . .
>
> Therefore, as God's chosen people, holy and dearly loved, clothe yourselves with compassion, kindness, humility, gentleness and patience. Bear with each other and forgive one another if any of you has a grievance against someone. Forgive as the Lord forgave you (Colossians 3:1–8, 12, 13).

Paul explains that when you live in a relationship with Jesus ("raised with Christ"), you will then grow to be more like Him. Remember, you do not grow by trying real hard to grow (hanging from the clothesline); you grow by eating. As you nurture your friendship with Jesus through Bible study, prayer, and serving others in His name, you become "hidden with Christ in God." As Paul explains in verse 4, Christ then becomes your life, and you live out Christ's glory. This glory is manifest through Christ in you living the sanctified life. This sanctified life is marked by the purging of anger, rage, malice, slander, and so on. Moreover, it is graced by compassion, kindness, humility, gentleness, and patience. But all of this is solely and fully the work of God; it is the act of grace.

Ken Canfield shares a beautiful picture of how this works:

> During a family vacation, Sarah got a little ornery and pushed Hannah.
> "Did you push your sister?" I asked.
> "No," she denied. Since this was becoming a growing pattern for Sarah, I decided to take a walk with her to get to the bottom of things.
> "Sarah," I told her, "I'm really disappointed with your behavior. What do you need to do about it?"
> I expected Sarah to tell me she needed to stop lying or apologize to her sister, but instead, with tears in her eyes, she said, "I need to ask Jesus to come into my heart."
> There I was, zeroing on behavior modification, and my 6-year-old daughter was dealing with the bigger issues of needing forgiveness, cleansing, and internal spiritual change. I was focused on morality, she on the spirituality that makes morality possible and sincere.[3]

Transformation, that is, "sanctification," does not happen by focusing on behavior modification. It is so much more than tweaking behavior. It is being in Christ and trusting Him with your power to choose how you will live.

So let's get a picture of what this looks like with skin on it. Think of it as the whole shebang in one life.

In 1731, William Cowper was born to an English clergyman and a mother with roots to prominent English royalty. Educated at Westminster School, he earned a law degree. He passed his bar examination and was licensed to practice as a solicitor in the lower courts of the English justice system.

In spite of his distinguished intellectual achievements, William Cowper was physically frail and emotionally volatile. One of the traumatic experiences that contributed to his instability was the death of his mother when he was only six years old. He could not stop grieving for his mother. This resulted in a mental breakdown from which he never recovered.

Consequently, he never practiced law. Contributing to his anxiety was an unhappy love affair that resulted in an unsuccessful suicide attempt. This landed William in an insane asylum for eighteen months.

In the asylum, he suffered from prolonged periods of deep depression. Much of his time there was spent in reading Scripture. One day, while reading the book of Romans, he was confronted with the words of the apostle Paul who said, "For all have sinned, and come short of the glory of God; being justified freely by his grace through the redemption that is in Christ Jesus: whom God hath set forth to be a propitiation through faith in his blood, to declare his righteousness for the remission of sins that are past, through the forbearance of God" (Romans 3:23–25, KJV).

Three words in one life: Cowper felt overwhelmed by the burden of guilt. His heart collided with grace in Romans 3:24, which declares that all guilty sinners are "justified freely by his grace through the redemption that is in Christ Jesus." Cowper then experienced the growth that inevitably occurs in the life of a redeemed sinner living in friendship with Jesus.

Upon his release from the institution, Cowper attended an Anglican church pastored by John Newton, the author of the hymn "Amazing Grace." With their combined efforts, Newton and Cowper would author 349 hymns. Among the sixty-seven hymns that Cowper wrote, the hymn that testifies of his final peace with his Savior has been called the redemptive anthem of the church. To this day, it stands as a monument to the sovereign grace of God. Cowper would later explain that it was while writing this hymn that he became aware of the efficacy of Christ's complete atonement for his sins.

Take your time and reflect deeply on the lyrics of that beloved hymn:

> There is a fountain filled with blood, drawn from Immanuel's veins,
> And sinners plunged beneath that flood lose all their guilty stains.
> The dying thief rejoiced to see that fountain in his day;
> And there have I, though vile as he, washed all my sins away.
> Dear dying Lamb, Thy precious blood shall never lose its pow'r,
> Till all the ransomed church of God are safe, to sin no more.
> E'er since by faith I saw the stream Thy flowing wounds supply,
> Redeeming love has been my theme, and shall be till I die.
> When this poor, lisping, stamm'ring tongue lies silent in the grave,
> Then in a nobler, sweeter song, I'll sing Thy pow'r to save.[4]

THE CLASSROOM

FIRST-GRADE ART

SECOND-GRADE COMPUTERS

 Elaine Creasman, on her Wordpress blog site, posts this insight: "Once we are saved, we are changed. I know my view of sin has changed even though I slip back into it. My attitude toward God has been rearranged even though I sometimes fail to obey Him. Before I knew Him, I was not bothered by my failure to do right. Now I am convicted and willing to be convinced to go His way.

"When I slip away from this sense that I am changed and being changed, it is because I back off from being in Christ. . . .

"There have been times when I've avoided looking at God—when I've stayed away from His Word and prayer out of hurt or disillusionment. But as I seek Him even in desperate times—especially in those times—I can sense a transformation taking place. He is changing me.[5]

Third-Grade Bible

"For everyone has sinned; we all fall short of God's glorious standard. Yet God, with undeserved kindness, declares that we are righteous. He did this through Christ Jesus when he freed us from the penalty for our sins" (Romans 3:23, 24, NLT).

"Every person has blown it—big time! Living up to God's holy standard is as likely as jumping to the moon. And even though we have done nothing to deserve it, God calls us saints, perfect, as if we had never sinned. The only reason God can get away with this is because He came to this earth and lived a perfect life for us and then He died to pay the penalty of sin. We get what Jesus deserves, and He takes the punishment that we deserve" (Romans 3:23, 24, our paraphrase).

Fourth-Grade Writing

J. I. Packer writes, "Were I asked to focus the New Testament message in three words, my proposal would be *adoption through propitiation,* and I do not expect ever to meet a richer or more pregnant summary of the gospel than that."[6]

Fifth-Grade Math

The gospel by numbers:
   A. People who have sinned = 100 percent
   B. People who are saved by their good deeds = 0 percent
   C. People who have accepted Christ's sacrifice on the cross who will be saved = 100 percent
   A + B = C

Endnotes

1. Michael Shermer, "Something Evil Comes This Way," Skeptic, accessed October 23, 2013, http://www.skeptic.com/eskeptic/04-03-18/.

2. Ellen G. White, *The Desire of Ages,* 25.

3. Ken Canfield, "The Heart of a Father," *Men of Integrity,* July 2001.

4. William Cowper, "There Is a Fountain," Timeless Truths, accessed July 26, 2013, http://library.timelesstruths.org/music/There_Is_a_Fountain/.

5. Elaine Creasman, "Changed," *Hearts Set Free* (blog), August 9, 2013, http://elainecreasman.wordpress.com/2013/08/09/changed/.

6. J. I. Packer, *Knowing God* (Downers Grove, IL: InterVarsity Press, 1993), 214; emphasis added.

– SUMMARY –
"...IFICATION" CLARIFICATION

So where have we been? Well, we have traversed the theological landscape of justification and sanctification, will and willpower, the fight of faith and the fight of sin, relational versus behavioral models of spirituality, righteousness, and faith and art and tweets and Peterbilts. Mostly, we've highlighted the imperative of a friendship with Jesus. Theologically speaking, everything hinges upon knowing Jesus personally through prayer, Bible study, and sharing.

Absolutely *everything*!

Things are different now than when we started this journey. While this book was being written, Morrie Venden passed away; Claire breezed through fifth grade and is now in seventh grade; and there's no question that I'm in a radically different place spiritually than I was at the outset. No book project has affected my life with God like this one. I pray that your testimony might be similar to mine.

The biggest game changer for me has been the realization that everything rests on the completed work of Jesus. Every season of salvation is Christ—not me—at work. While I heard Pastor Venden share these ideas back in the seventies when I was in fifth grade, only now have I come to understand that justification, sanctification, and glorification are all and equally the work of grace.

At the outset of the Week of Spiritual Emphasis back at Andrews University, Pastor Venden explained, "There are three aspects of salvation. Salvation from our past sins—we call it justification. Salvation from our present sinning—we call this sanctification. Salvation from a world of sin when Jesus comes again—we call this glorification. The process by which all three of them happen is exactly the same."

Now we have no trouble with number one, justification. Salvation, forgiveness for our past sins, we have no problem accepting that. There is nothing we can do; all we can do is come to Christ just as we are. And we have no hang-ups with number three, salvation from this world of sin. There is nothing we can do to go from earth to heaven. It takes a lot of power even to get to the moon, let alone to heaven. We must have the power of God to transplant us from this planet to the heavenly country. There is nothing we can do but rely totally upon Him.

But somehow we have gotten the idea that in sanctification, the middle aspect of salvation, that it is faith plus effort, faith plus works. Colossians 2:6 says, "As ye have therefore received Christ Jesus the Lord, so walk ye in him" (KJV). *Steps to Christ* in commenting on that verse says, "Do you ask, 'How am I to abide in Christ?' In the same way as you received Him at first."[1] *"In the same way"*—we are to grow into the character of Christ and live in Him; transformation happens in the same way that we are saved in the first place. In other words, we are sanctified by grace alone; it is God who is responsible for our life change.

Ellen White (with my notes inserted) writes, "Divine grace is needed at the beginning [that is, *justification*], divine grace at every step of advance [*sanctification*], and divine grace alone can complete the work [*glorification*]."[2]

In the words of author Harry Blamires, "In the Christian life, nothing, nothing at all, can be purchased at the do-it-yourself shop." It is *all* the work of Jesus.

So now let's consider each season of salvation, saving the sticky subject of sanctification for last.

JUSTIFICATION *BY FAITH* ALONE

Romans 3:21–24 is clear:

> But now apart from the law the righteousness of God has been made known, to which the Law and the Prophets testify. This righteousness is given through faith in Jesus Christ to all who believe. There is no difference between Jew and Gentile, for all have sinned and fall short of the glory of God, and all are justified freely by his grace through the redemption that came by Christ Jesus.

Justification, or right standing before God, comes freely by grace alone. There is no way you can make yourself right apart from Christ.

Sarah "Fergie" Ferguson, the English ex-royal, knows all about the futility of trying to make herself right. A favorite fodder for the tabloids, the red-haired former Duchess of York was married to Prince Andrew, the second son of Queen Elizabeth, from 1986 until they divorced in 1996.

Fergie's life has been a series of missteps and scandals. Her Wikipedia biography reports, "By 1991, the marriage was in trouble, and the couple had drifted apart. While her husband was away on naval or royal duties, the Duchess was frequently seen in the company of other men. . . . After four years of official separation, the Duke and Duchess announced the mutual decision to divorce in May 1996."[3]

Other scandals are referenced as well. A 2010 article about Sarah in *The Week* reported that she was caught trying to sell access to her former husband for forty thousand dollars. On January 13, 2012, the Ministry of Justice of the Republic of Turkey issued an international arrest warrant for Fergie for allegedly making a false declaration when entering the country, trespassing into a Turkish government institution, and violating the privacy of children. And, of course, the world noticed when she got the royal snub of the century: she was not among the nineteen hundred people invited to the 2011 royal wedding of Prince William and Kate Middleton.

Sarah did watch the wedding. Referring to Kate's wedding walk at Westminster Abbey, retracing the steps that she herself had taken in 1986, Sarah reflected, "With [Kate] going up the aisle, you know what went through my head? . . . I feel like I've handed her the baton and said: 'Well done. And you'll do it right.' I didn't do it right, and now I am going to go get *Sarah* right."[4]

In that respect, we can all identify with Fergie, can't we? Sooner or later, we all see that we've botched things up royally and not only do we need to fix the situation, we need to fix ourselves. Which begs the question: What do you do when you decide you're going to go get yourself right? How do you do that?

Paul tells us that "rightness" is not something we do through our ingenuity and grit, but rather it is a gift "given through faith in Jesus Christ to all who believe" (verse 22). You will never be strong enough, smart enough, or spiritual enough to fix your faulty standing before God. Trusting fully and only in Jesus—there is no other way to be right with God.

Nathan Cole, a Connecticut farmer who converted to Jesus Christ in the 1740s, described what happened to him when he received this gift of salvation: "My hearing [the good news of Jesus] gave me a heart wound. By God's blessing, my old foundation was broken up, and I saw that my righteousness would not save me."

My righteousness will not save me. Your righteousness will not save you. Right standing with God is something given to us; never is it earned.

GLORIFICATION BY FAITH ALONE

The other spiritual reality that sandwiches transformation is glorification— redemption from this world of sin when Jesus comes again. The Bible tells us that we will be glorified "in a flash, in the twinkling of an eye, at the last trumpet. For the trumpet will sound, the dead will be raised imperishable, and we will be changed" (1 Corinthians 15:52).

Note that the text does not teach that we will change ourselves in that moment and wing our way to heaven by our fervent flapping. No, "we will be changed." It is God who is the Agent of change, and it is He who is responsible for transporting us from this world to the next.

Not many folk have a problem accepting the fact that we can't fly to heaven in our own power. We understand our limitations on this one, right?

As a child, my favorite place to visit was Grandpa's house in College Place, Washington. Among other attractions, there was an old barn toward the back of his property. One summer afternoon, I climbed up on that roof with my brother Paul.

Handing him an umbrella, I asked, "Have you ever wanted to fly like Mary Poppins?"

Of course, he wanted to fly!

"You can!" I promised. "Just go up to the peak of the roof and get a running start. Hang on real tightly to the umbrella, and you'll soar around town like a bird."

"Really?" He had his doubts, but he assumed his older brother was all knowing about such things. "Are you absolutely, positively, 100 percent sure that I will fly?"

"Scout's honor," I said with my fingers discreetly crossed behind my back.

Climbing to the ridge on the roof, he gripped the umbrella and started his countdown to glory. "Ten, nine, eight, seven, six, five, four—"

Peering over the edge, he wanted some reassurance. "Have you ever done this? Are you sure this umbrella will make me fly like Mary Poppins?"

"Of course, I'm sure! I'm your brother! Would I ever steer you wrong?" In short order, his answer to that question was about to change.

"OK," he said as he finished the countdown.

"Three, two, one!"

He raced down the roof and jumped high into the air, clutching that umbrella like his life depended on it.

Guess what? Paul can't fly. What works for Mary Poppins doesn't work for the common man.

In case you're curious about what happened to Paul, I'm happy to report that no sibling was injured in the making of this story. It was not a high roof, and piled below was a sizable mound of cornstalks that provided an ideal landing spot. We discovered that jumping off the roof was the perfect summer afternoon activity. Of course, we scrapped the umbrella for all future flights.

Now I suppose some folk embrace Mary Poppins's theology, thinking they will soar some day to heaven by their own power and hard work. But most of us understand that the fanciest umbrella we can find is an utterly useless prop when it comes to flying. And the finest works we can muster are futile when it comes to being glorified from this world to the next.

"Heaven goes by favor," Mark Twain famously quipped. "If it went by merit, you would stay out, and your dog would go in."

We aren't getting into heaven by our merits. Glorification will happen only by the unmerited favor of God.

Sanctification *by Faith* Alone

Now let's tackle the tricky one—sanctification. Here's where we want to believe that our efforts are required; transformation into the character of Christ happens by grace *and* works, right? Or does it?

Philippians 2:13 tells us, "For God is working in you, giving you the desire and the power to do what pleases him" (NLT). Notice it does not suggest that you are doing the work; rather, God is doing the work, and He is changing your desires and supplying all the power to do His will. God is the active Agent in this adventure of sanctification, not you.

Ephesians 4:21–24 puts it like this: "Since you have heard about Jesus and have learned the truth that comes from him, throw off your old sinful nature and your former way of life, which is corrupted by lust and deception. Instead, let the Spirit renew your thoughts and attitudes. Put on your new nature, created to be like God—truly righteous and holy" (NLT). Paul calls us to allow the Spirit to make this change within. Sanctification—this process of throwing off the old sinful nature and putting on the new, righteous, and holy nature—is God's work, not ours.

Jesus was clear: "I am the vine; you are the branches. If you remain in me and I in you, you will bear much fruit; apart from me you can do nothing" (John 15:5). Apart from Jesus we are helpless to bear fruit.

For many years, I preached and wrote about the importance of training rather than trying in the spiritual life. Consider this case in point from my book published in 1999:

> Paul states very forcefully that we can be freed from . . . sin. How? By staying fully connected to Christ—in His death and His resurrection. As we live in the presence of Jesus, we are granted the grace to experience freedom from sin, for sin cannot coexist in the presence of God.
>
> That's why our attempts to try and stop sinning in our own power are so futile. Sin is stronger than willpower. Freedom from sin comes not in *trying* but in *training*. Through a regimen of training disciplines (such as prayer, fasting, corporate worship, solitude, etc.) that catapult us into the presence of God, we are changed internally. Ultimately, the external guise is transformed as well.

John Ortberg's testimony rings familiar for many of us who wrestle with sin.

> For much of my life, when I heard messages about following Jesus, I thought in terms of trying hard to be like him. So after hearing (or preaching, for that matter) a sermon on patience on Sunday, I would wake up Monday morning determined to be a more patient person. Have you ever tried to be patient with a three-year-old? I have—and it generally didn't work any better than would my trying hard to run a marathon for which I had not trained. I would end up exhausted and defeated. Given the way we are prone to describe "following Jesus," it's a wonder anyone wants to do it at all.
>
> Spiritual transformation is not a matter of trying harder, but of training wisely. This is what the apostle Paul means when he encourages his young protégé Timothy to "train yourself in godliness."[5]

While I would not suggest that I was wrong in highlighting the difference between trying and training, it seems that this teaching is incomplete. After reading from one of John Ortberg's books on this topic, I decided that I would follow his suggestion and enter God's "University of Sanctification" for the day; I would train to become a more patient person. So I prayed, "God, I am tired of trying to be a more patient person. I get short with church members, I snap at my kids, and I push the elevator button a dozen times before it comes (even though I know that doesn't help!). I am so impatient! God, I know that the only way I will ever change is by training. So I give You this day to put me in situations where I learn patience."

God answered my prayer.

Later that morning, I was in line at the post office. The gentleman in front of me wanted to put his mail on hold indefinitely.

"We can't do that," the lady behind the counter explained. "We can only hold your mail for thirty days."

"But I need forever, not thirty days," the man said in broken English.

"You need to get a post office box here," she said.

"No, I can no afford," he said.

Meanwhile, I'm next in line waiting patiently. I recognized the situation immediately as God's tutoring. He was transforming me into a more patient person. So I used the time to pray.

Thank You, God, for answering my prayer, I thought. *I know You are teaching me patience—a virtue I definitely lack. I'm done* trying *to be more patient. I see that You are training me to be more patient.*

The argument between the clerk and the customer stretched into fifteen minutes. Thirty minutes. Forty-five minutes.

God, I prayed, *must You start me with a graduate level course? Patience 101 was more the level I had in mind.* But I was still relatively chill. This training was necessary in my quest to become a better Christian.

By this point, the line behind me spilled outside the post office, stretching the length of the sidewalk around the building. No sweat; I had prayed for training in patience, and I was getting it.

Only then did it dawn on me that I had forgotten my wallet and left it at home. Just as the man was leaving, I dropped from the line to retrieve my wallet. At this point, there was not a happy thought anywhere in my mind. In that moment, I had the patience of a starving lion at Golden Corral. "Patience, schmatience!" I fumed. "I wasted my morning!"

"The litmus test of whether or not you understand the gospel is what you do when you fail," asserts Pastor Matt Chandler. "Do you run from God and go try to clean yourself up a bit before you come back into the throne room, or do you approach the throne of grace with confidence? If you don't approach the throne of grace with confidence, you don't understand the gospel. You are most offensive to God when you come to him with all of your efforts, when you're still trying to earn what's freely given."[6]

I wondered, *How many times have I offended God when trying to earn what is freely given?* The limitations of training began to dawn on me. No, trying hard will not work. Yes, training is important. But what I was missing all those years in my understanding of how sanctification works is the third and most critical option: trusting. Nowadays, I am preaching that it's not about trying, and it's not just about training; ultimately, it is all about trusting God to change me into the new creation that He wants to be.

The morning after my post office fiasco, I read this statement by W. W. Prescott: "For a long time I tried to gain the victory over sin, but I failed. I have since learned the reason. Instead of doing the part which God expects me to do, and which I can do, I was trying to do God's part, which He does not expect me to do, and which I cannot do. Primarily, my part is . . . to receive the victory."[7]

I had to reread that a few times to digest what he was saying. *"I tried to gain the victory over sin, but I failed"*—yep, that was definitely my story. And he claims to have discovered the reason for this? I had to know why.

"Instead of doing the part which God expects me to do, and which I can do." What is this part that only I can do and God cannot do for me? Surrender. Trust Him with my power to choose. Allow Him to drive.

"I was trying to do God's part, which He does not expect me to do, and which I cannot do." And what is God's part that I cannot do? Sanctification! Overcoming sin. Changing me into a new creation.

Posting the quote on Facebook, I added this reflection: " 'If anyone is in Christ he is a new creature.' I have been trying harder to be a new creature than I have been trying to be in Christ. Don't fight sin. Find Christ."

I hope you caught that. *Don't fight sin. Find Christ.*

Tullian Tchividjian adds this: "God does not move us *beyond* the gospel; he moves us more deeply *into* the gospel, because all of the power we need in order to change and mature comes *through* the gospel. . . . The gospel does not simply ignite the Christian life; it is the fuel that keeps Christians going and growing every day. Real change cannot come apart from the gospel.[8]

It is divine grace—the gospel—that fuels all change in the Christian's life. OK, but what do we do then with the numerous statements in Scripture that command us to "make every effort"?

For example, Jesus said, "Make every effort to enter through the narrow door, because many, I tell you, will try to enter and will not be able to" (Luke 13:24). Using the metaphor of a narrow door for salvation, Jesus tells us to "make every effort" to get through it. Clearly, He is telling us to work hard at securing our salvation, right? Then Jesus says, "Once the owner of the house gets up and closes the door, you will stand outside knocking and pleading, 'Sir, open the door for us' " (verse 25).

We are quick to apply this text and say, "Better work hard to get through that door. If you don't, Jesus slams it shut, and you will be lost. Salvation comes only to those who 'make every effort' to earn it." But is that what Jesus is really saying?

Notice where we must focus our effort. When the owner closes the door, he gives this reason: "I don't know you" (verse 25).

The effort is always focused on knowing Jesus. Our singular obsession in the Christian life must be on knowing Him. Personally. Intimately. Do that, and you will be saved. You see, the Bible is not opposed to making an effort in salvation; but it speaks forcefully against trying to earn salvation. So work on knowing Jesus, not on cleaning up your sins so you can squeeze through the narrow door. Remember, it's about effort, not earning.

This week, my wife and I will celebrate our twenty-seventh anniversary. I would be lying if I suggested that there has been no effort in keeping our marriage together. Relationships require work. But I need not obsess over my marital status. Effort to earn my standing as a husband in my marital relationship would be misguided. I am very secure in my status as a husband. But being a good husband takes work—a lot of it! My effort, of course, is always invested in nurturing our relationship, not proving that we are legally married.

Peter explains, "Everything that goes into a life of pleasing God has been miraculously given to us by getting to know, personally and intimately, the One who invited us to God" (2 Peter 1:3, *The Message*). The Web site New Bible.com offers this commentary: "He has given us everything we need for a Godly life. God is not stingy. He desires to give. He has given everything! Whatever is His is ours. BY KNOWING HIM! It's not enough to know the right things about God, demons in hell know the right things about God. This is about a relationship, an intimate knowledge of God—not an acquaintance; but KNOWING.[9]

Peter then challenges us to "make every effort" (verse 5), and he describes the process of sanctification. But notice that each component of this transformed life (that is, the sanctified life) is built upon one thing—*faith*. Righteousness is built on the foundation of faith in Jesus. Consider Peter's counsel to "make every effort to add to your faith goodness; and to goodness, knowledge; and to knowledge, self-control; and to self-control, perseverance; and to perseverance, godliness; and to godliness, mutual affection; and to mutual affection, love. For if you possess these qualities in increasing measure, they will keep you from being ineffective and unproductive in your knowledge of our Lord Jesus Christ" (2 Peter 1:5–8).

So clearly, we are called to manifest the fruits of the Spirit and to grow in grace; but this transformation in our lives is the work of God through faith in Jesus. "These qualities," Peter concludes, "will keep you from being ineffective and unproductive in your knowledge of our Lord Jesus Christ." Once again, sanctification comes back to knowing Jesus Christ. Peter adds in the next verse, "But whoever does not have . . . [these attributes of sanctification] is nearsighted and blind, forgetting that they have been cleansed from their past sins" (verse 9).

This reference "cleansed from their past sins" clearly speaks to the work of justification. But again, we must underscore that we do not cleanse ourselves from past sins, rather we "have been cleansed" from our past grievances against God by

His grace. Justification is His work.

Then Peter makes a reference to glorification when he repeats the command to "make every effort." He concludes, "Therefore, my brothers and sisters, make every effort to confirm your calling and election. For if you do these things, you will never stumble, and you will receive a rich welcome into the eternal kingdom of our Lord and Savior Jesus Christ" (verses 10, 11).

Stay with Jesus and you will be glorified. By His grace you "*will* receive a rich welcome into the eternal kingdom."

Paul reinforces Peter's contention that every season of salvation is a gift from God. "It is because of him that you are in Christ Jesus, who has become for us wisdom from God—that is, our righteousness [*justification*], holiness [*sanctification*] and redemption [*glorification*]. Therefore, as it is written: 'Let the one who boasts boast in the Lord' " (1 Corinthians 1:30, 31).

Here's the bottom line: it's all about Jesus. By faith in Jesus, we are saved. By faith in Jesus, we are changed. By faith in Jesus, we will be glorified.

It's Jesus.

Jesus only.

Jesus all.

Jesus. Period.

Jesus. The beginning. The end. And everything in between.

It's *all* about Jesus.

Amen.

ENDNOTES

1. Ellen G. White, *Steps to Christ*, 69.

2. Ellen G. White, *Testimonies to Ministers and Gospel Workers* (Mountain View, CA: Pacific Press®, 1962), 508.

3. Wikipedia contributors, "Sarah, Duchess of York," Wikipedia, accessed July 29, 2013, http://en.wikipedia.org/wiki/Sarah,_Duchess_of_York.

4. Laura M. Holson, "Saving Sarah From Herself, Oprah Style," *New York Times*, June 3, 2011, http://www.nytimes.com/2011/06/05/fashion/sarah-fergusons-transformation.html?pagewanted=all&_r=0.

5. John Ortberg, *The Life You've Always Wanted* (Grand Rapids, MI: Zondervan Publishing House, 1997), 47.

6. Matt Chandler, "Remembering Your Creator," Preaching Today, accessed October 24, 2013, http://www.preachingtoday.com/illustrations/2011/october/3102411.html.

7. W. W. Prescott, *Victory in Christ* (Washington, DC: Review and Herald®, n.d.), 17.

8. Tullian Tchividjian, "Trusting in God's Declaration," PreachingToday, accessed October 24, 2013, http://www.preachingtoday.com/sermons/sermons/2012/june/godsdeclaration.html.

9. "Know," New Bible.com, accessed August 12, 2013 https://www.bible.com/notes/50090.

– APPENDIX A –

WANNA KEEP GROWING?

"So this year's gonna be different," you sigh to yourself after an amazing Week of Prayer. "I'm going to be more spiritual than Enoch."

Fat chance.

OK, how about this: "I'm just going to grow spiritually—a teensy-weensy little bit each day."

Yep, that works. But what's your game plan? If you are serious about spiritual growth in the new year, you can't just whistle along and hope it happens. So check out this GPS (God's planning strategy) unit. To stay on course, put it on the dashboard of your car or on your refrigerator where you can review it every morning.

EVERY DAY: GET AN STP TREATMENT

Check out the Web site www.STP.com, and you'll see their pitch: "From 1954 to today, STP® products are specially formulated to help you get the most out of your vehicle." Similarly, if you're interested in getting the most out of your friendship with Jesus, then remember STP. Do these three things every day.

"S"–STUDY

First, study the Word. Richard Foster writes,

> Many Christians remain in bondage to fears and anxieties simply because they do not avail themselves of the Discipline of study. They may be faithful in church attendance and earnest in fulfilling their religious duties, and still they are not changed. . . . They may sing with gusto, pray in the Spirit, live as obediently as they know, even receive divine visions and revelations, and yet the tenor of their lives remains unchanged. Why? Because they have never taken up one of the central ways God uses to change us: study.[1]

"T"–TELL OTHERS

In the words of Donald Miller, "I used to say that I believed it was important to tell people about Jesus, but I never did. [My friend] Andrew very kindly explained that if I do not introduce people to Jesus, then I don't believe Jesus is an important person. It doesn't matter what I say."[2]

Share the gospel with someone, in some way, every day. Share your Friend with your friends.

"P"–PRAY

Ellen White reminds us, "Prayer is the opening of the heart to God as to a friend."[3] So every day, pour out your heart to your Friend. Tell Him about your hang-ups when you're doing homework; sing Him a prayer when you're struck by the splendor of a sunset; talk to Him when you're waiting at the drive-through. "Pray without ceasing" (1 Thessalonians 5:17, KJV).

EVERY WEEK: CELEBRATE SABBATH

Rabbi Abraham Heschel writes, "In the tempestuous ocean of time and toil there are islands of stillness where man may enter a harbor and reclaim his dignity. The island is the seventh day, the Sabbath, a day of detachment from things, instruments and practical affairs as well as of attachment to the spirit."[4]

The Sabbath provides an opportunity every week to grow your relationship with God. How? The possibilities are endless, but here are twenty-one Sabbath activities to get you started:

1. Walk to church (at least park a few blocks from your church and walk that far).
2. Make a top-ten list of things that make you feel happy.
3. Write a letter to an old friend who'll be shocked to hear from you.
4. Pass out biscuits to neighborhood dogs.
5. Read a book about a missionary.
6. Learn about a Jewish feast or custom and try doing it.
7. Fly a kite.
8. Feed the ducks.
9. Host a contest with your friends to see who can find the strangest story in Scripture (there are some doozies in 1 and 2 Samuel).
10. Visit the Humane Society, adopt the mangiest animal, and give it as a gift to someone you don't like. (I'm not kidding—about the first part.)
11. Take a long bath.
12. Compile a list of questions you'd like to ask Jesus.
13. Watch kids play.
14. Read the last chapter of *The Great Controversy*, and talk to God about your hopes for the future.
15. Reflect on the greatest miracle in your life.
16. Play charades.

APPENDIX A - 153

17. Learn a new hymn.
18. Write your own translation of the book of James.
19. Make a list of twenty-five things Daniel may have been thinking in the lions' den.
20. Answer the phone with "Happy Sabbath."
21. Sabbath by Sabbath, cross off whatever items on this list that you do; see how many weeks it takes you to do all of them.

EVERY QUARTER: GO FAST

Every quarter (perhaps when your church celebrates Communion), practice the discipline of fasting. Perhaps the first quarter you will choose to go a day without food. The second quarter of the year, try to refrain for a week from social networking—no texting, Myspacing, Tweeting, or Facebooking. Third quarter, maybe spend a month fasting from television. Polish off the year by fasting for the entire quarter from refined sugar or deep-fried foods.

EVERY YEAR: ESCAPE

Carve a couple of days out of your calendar where you can be alone with God. "Without solitude," says Henri Nouwen, "it is virtually impossible to live a spiritual life."[5]

So you want to keep your relationship with God strong? You absolutely can! You got a plan. Now, execute the plan.

ENDNOTES

1. Richard Foster, *Celebration of Discipline* (New York: Harper & Row, 1978), 54.
2. Donald Miller, *Blue Like Jazz* (Nashville, Thomas Nelson, 2003), 110.
3. Ellen G. White, *Steps to Christ*, 93.
4. Abraham Heschel, *The Sabbath* (New York: Farrar, Straus and Girous, 1951), 29.
5. Henri Nouwen, *Making All Things New* (New York : HarperCollins, 1981), 69.

– APPENDIX B –

KARL'S COMMANDMENTS FOR BIBLE STUDY

A circuit-riding preacher entered a church building with his young son and dropped a coin into the offering box in the back. Not many came that Sunday, and those who did didn't seem too excited about what was preached. After the service, the preacher and son walked to the back. He emptied the box to discover that only one coin fell out. "Dad," the boy said, "if you'd have put more in, you'd have gotten more out!"

That statement is especially true when it comes to studying the Bible. The more you put into it, the more you get out of it. But what does "putting more into it" mean? Here are ten suggestions.

1. Submit to the Spirit. Before diving into the Word, ask God to guide you. Don't forget that spiritual things are spiritually discerned (1 Corinthians 2:14).

2. Enter the time machine. It's helpful to cross the barrier of time to understand the people of the Bible and their culture. The more you learn about the context in which the events and conversations of Scripture took place, the more meaningful your Bible study can become.

3. Learn the language. Because the Bible was written in Hebrew, Aramaic, and Greek, there is a barrier to understanding its message. Fortunately, language experts have bridged this gap for us by offering modern translations in English. Still, it's helpful to explore the original meanings and words. You can do this with the help of commentaries and numerous Web sites.

4. Start with a summary. First, get an overview of the entire book that you're studying. In this way, you can get a feel for overarching ideas and repeated themes.

5. Outline the passage. Break down the flow of the section you're studying by inserting titles and subtitles into the text.

6. Consider context. Look at the passages immediately before and after the verses that you're studying. Ask yourself, What is the main idea that the author was trying to communicate?

7. Put yourself in the story. To make Bible study come alive, imagine yourself in the situation. Picture yourself cramped in a smelly den of lions or taking that first step out of the boat to walk on water or in the pit wondering if your brothers will kill you.

8. Reflect on what you read. Listen to Ellen White's counsel: "Scripture must be compared with scripture. There must be careful research and prayerful reflection."[1]

9. Apply what you learn today! The quality of your study is ultimately measured by how much you allow it to shape your life. The goal is to have the character of Christ formed within you. If that's not happening, then you're not getting much out of your study.

10. Practice. Practice. Practice. Studying the Bible is like any other skill—the more you do it, the easier it becomes. So stick with it!

Well, now you know Karl's "Commandments for Studying the Bible." Give them a try. It's like putting money in your bank.

ENDNOTE

1. Ellen G. White, *Steps to Christ,* 90, 91.

– APPENDIX C –

HOW TO PRAY

"One day Jesus was praying in a certain place. When he finished, one of his disciples said to him, 'Lord, teach us to pray' " (Luke 11:1).

Have you ever caught yourself mindlessly babbling a prayer that never treks through the brain? For example, someone sits in front of a nutritional disaster—a plate piled with deep-fried fat that's loaded with sugar and slathered in butter, and how does the prayer go? "Dear God, help this food to nourish my body so I can do Your will."

You don't need to pray for God's will in that moment. His will would be for you to push away from the table and feed the garbage to the dog. Except God loves dogs, so He'd prefer you give it to the cat. (Note to cat lovers: I'm joking! Do not, I repeat, *do not* send me hate mail!)

Jesus longs to hear the honest prayers of His children. Jesus makes this clear in Matthew 6 with three in-your-face statements—all of them negative—that provide keys to a satisfying and God-honoring prayer life. Take a few minutes and read Matthew 6. Then read this summary.

1. Don't be hypocritical (verses 1, 2, 5, 16). Jesus despised meaningless God-talk and pious-sounding clichés. Jesus cherished simple, sincere sinners who approached Him with every wart exposed. Robert Murray M'Cheyne suggests, "What a person is on his knees before God, that he is, and nothing more." If you're angry with God, tell Him so. If you're disappointed, pray about it. If you're scared, let Him know. Be real with God.

2. Don't use meaningless repetition (verses 7, 8). The evangelist Dwight L. Moody, was once seized with the realization of how much God had blessed him. Interrupting his eloquent prayer, he shouted, "Stop, God!" What a welcome slice of spontaneity! It's a nice change from "Eternal, Almighty, All-gracious Father of all life, Thy hand hath wonderfully and graciously provided allest of minest needs . . . ," and on and on, grinding into snore city. Martin Luther had it right: "The fewer words the better prayer." I've heard it said, "Don't use a gallon of words to express a spoonful of thoughts."

3. Don't ask for mercy from God until you show mercy to others (verses 14, 15).

Norman Vincent Peale once told a story from his childhood. When he was a boy, he found a big, black cigar. Slipping into an alley, he lit up. It didn't taste good, but it made him feel very grown up—until he saw his father coming. Quickly, he put the cigar behind his back and tried to be casual.

Desperate to divert his father's attention, Norman pointed to a billboard advertising the circus. "Can I go, Dad? Please, let's go when it comes to town."

His father's reply taught Norman a lesson he never forgot. "Son," he said, "never make a petition while at the same time trying to hide a smoldering disobedience."[1]

A friend once told me, "Since the lines have been cleared between the Lord and me, the telephone has never stopped ringing."

So clear up the lines and pray. "Pray all the time" (1 Thessalonians 5:17, *The Message*). Pray while you're exercising. Pray in the shower. Pray while you're watching TV. You should even pray before you eat—which might just make your cat fat.

ENDNOTE

1. "Norman Vincent Peale," SermonSearch, accessed October 24, 2013, http://www.sermonsearch.com/sermon-illustrations/4915/norman-vincent-peale/.

— APPENDIX D —

WINNING YOUR WORLD FOR JESUS

Christian comedian Ken Davis tells a delightful story of Beth, a.k.a. "Space Cadet." Ken admits, "She was the ditziest person I've ever seen in my life." Nevertheless, she responded to Ken's challenge to be involved with their campus ministry program known as Youth for Christ, or YFC.

The premise in YFC was that students make the best evangelists. Because students regularly interface with their peers, YFC taught that the young people could witness more effectively than pastors, teachers, or even professional evangelists.

One evening, Ken revved up the students with an evangelism pep talk. "You are God's answer to reach the lost students in your high school," he preached. "You have access. You have their ear. You have their respect. You are their age. So go and reach your lost friends for Jesus!"

Following the meeting, Beth approached Ken. "Oh, Pastor," she sobbed, "I, um, ah, well, I want to share Jesus with my friends, but, ah, I don't know what to say."

"Relax," Ken consoled. "Beth, God will tell you what to say."

"Well," she cried, "I don't know where to start."

"Listen, why don't you go home tonight and pray that God will lay on your heart one person. Pick that friend to share your faith with. Just one, Beth, start there."

Abruptly, the tears stopped. "Oh," she giggled. "OK."

So she prayed. God laid someone on her heart. And she invited her friend to the YFC meeting. Outfitted for battle, Beth carried a tract in her pocket that explained the miracle of salvation. For the entire evening, the pamphlet was burning a hole in her pocket. She was waiting for that moment when she could whip it out and do the thing we call witnessing.

On the way home, Beth's heart was pounding like a spastic woodpecker. It was witness time! Casually, she asked her friend, "So, what did you think of the meeting tonight?"

"Well," her friend replied, "I liked it except for the Jesus part."

Ouchie! Beth thought. *It's the Jesus part that I got in my pocket. Now what am I going to do?*

Collecting her wits, Beth responded, "What didn't you like about the Jesus part?"

The question prompted a sordid testimony shadowed by shame. Then her friend asked, "How could Jesus ever forgive me after all that I've done?"

Beth reckoned she would save witnessing for later. She pulled the car over and began to tell the story of her life. She also spoke of guilt and pain, but her story was punctuated with a sense of hope, because she knew that Jesus had completely forgiven her.

At the end of the conversation, Beth's friend said, "Could you show me please how I could come to peace with my past?" Beth introduced her to Christ— without ever opening the pamphlet.

The next Monday, Beth shared her story with Pastor Ken. By the end of the story, she started crying. "Beth," he said, "what's the matter? This is a reason for joy."

"No, now I don't have anybody to witness to. What am I going to do now?" she said.

"Beth, relax! Pick another friend."

Once again, the tears stopped abruptly. "Oh," she giggled. "OK."

Her senior year in high school, Beth led seven kids into saving relationships with Jesus Christ. And to think, she never did know what to say! Nevertheless, Beth changed her little world by sharing Jesus.

Sometimes all the talk about "winning our cities for Christ" and "global mission" and "reaching the world" can sound so intimidating, not too mention far-fetched. Amid the lofty dreams and dialogue, let's not forget that evangelism always boils down to a simple definition: it's one beggar telling another beggar where to find bread. It's about you and me and young people such as Beth being intentional about sharing with lost people what Jesus means to us. It's eating every day in our personal devotional time with the Living Bread, and then we have food to share with friends. When we all sign on to do that, I believe we're well on our way to winning the world for Jesus.

The Three Habits of Highly Holy Christians

Aristotle once said, "Good habits formed at youth make all the difference."

Other wise guys have agreed. In Scripture, we're urged to form three habits of holiness that dramatically impact the spiritual life. What are these habits?

First, the habit of prayer: "Steadfastly maintain the *habit* of prayer" (Romans 12:12, Phillips; emphasis added).

Mother Teresa once said: "Prayer enlarges the heart until it is capable of containing God's gift of himself." It's no wonder she would often spend hours in prayer.

News anchor Dan Rather once asked Mother Teresa, "What do you say to God when you pray?"

"I listen," said Mother Teresa.

"And what does God say to you?"

"He listens."

Prayer, in its purest form, is simply being in the presence of Jesus.

Second, the habit of study: "The man who looks into the perfect mirror of God's law . . . and makes a *habit* of so doing, is not the man who sees and forgets. He puts that law into practice and he wins true happiness" (James 1:25, Phillips; emphasis added).

Max Lucado illustrates this by a scene from a school cafeteria. Imagine selecting your entrée and your salad, but when you get to the vegetables, you see something that looks too gross for a stint on *Fear Factor*.

"What is that nastiness?" you ask, pointing.

"Oh, don't ask," replies the embarrassed server behind the counter.

"What is it?" you persist.

"Well, if you must know, it's a pan of pre-chewed food."

"Huh?"

"Pre-chewed food. Some people prefer to swallow what others have chewed."

Lucado comments,

Repulsive? You bet. But widespread. More so than you might imagine. Not with cafeteria food, but with God's Word.

Such Christians mean well. They listen well. But they discern little. They are content to swallow whatever they are told. No wonder they've stopped growing.[1]

Third, the habit of fellowship: "Let us not give up the *habit* of meeting together, as some are doing. Instead, let us encourage one another" (Hebrews 10:25, TEV; emphasis added).

I'm often anguished at how casual people tend to be about the church. Many people view church as just another option on the weekend. Go hiking in the mountains, stay in my room and play video games, meet some friends at Denny's, catch up on sleep, go to church—whatever suits my fancy.

As Joshua Harris puts it, we prefer to "date" the church. We certainly don't care to commit to the church like the Bridegroom commits to His bride. Harris writes, "We are a generation of consumers, independent and critical. We attend church, but we don't want to settle down and truly invest ourselves. We're not into commitment—we only want to *date* the church."[2]

This dater's mind-set is not biblical. God established the church, He died for the church, and He continues to sustain the church. The church deal is a big deal to God. No wonder He exhorts us to "not give up the habit" of attending church.

So there you have it: three habits of highly holy Christians. Now go practice.

ENDNOTES ────────────

1. Max Lucado, *When God Whispers Your Name* (Dallas: Word Publishing), 144.

2. Joshua Harris, *Stop Dating the Church* (Colorado Springs, CO: Multnomah Publishing), back cover.

CLASS DISCUSSIONS

– GOD IN A BOX –

1. If your house were on fire and you could save only one box of stuff, what would you keep and why?

2. How would you describe to an atheist friend what you value most in life? Would your description change if you were talking to a Christian friend? Why or why not?

3. With whom do you identify most in the story of the prodigal son? Why?

   • The prodigal son
   • The elder brother
   • The father
   • The fattened calf

4. Where would you rank yourself on the continuum below to describe your understanding of faith?

Behavior (-10) _____ 0 _____ (10) Relationship

5. Were you taught to think about sin primarily as a bad behavior or as a broken relationship? Explain.

6. What are the essential beliefs and practices of Christian faith?

7. How do you cultivate the practice of a "habitual, silent, secret conversation of the soul with God"?

– WHEN GOD GAGS –

1. Complete the sentence: "I'd give anything to meet . . ." Share why.

2. Describe your experiences with the church as a child. Do you think the church today is healthier than the church of your childhood? About the same? Less healthy? Why?

3. Read the "Seven Woes on the Teachers of the Law and the Pharisees" in Matthew 23. What do you think God sees as the primary evil of the Pharisees? How are the followers of Jesus to avoid the same pitfalls today? What is the primary difference between the Pharisees and true followers of Jesus?

4. Have you ever recognized a spirit of self-sufficiency ("I don't need . . .") in yourself? How about a spirit of apathy ("I don't care . . .")? How do these attitudes affect one's spiritual walk?

5. In Satan's efforts to derail Christians today, what do you think is a more effective tool—an attitude of self-sufficiency or an attitude of apathy? Which attitude seems most prevalent in the church today? Why?

6. How are the sins of self-sufficiency and apathy similar? How are they different?

7. Do you think the church has a realistic view of its true condition today? How do you think the church is the same and/or different from Laodicea? Explain.

8. If Jesus took your spiritual temperature today, what would it be? What would be the spiritual temperature in your local church?

9. Share from your experience some practical ways that you can open the door of your heart and invite Jesus to come in and eat with you.

– "A QUARTERBACK AND A COACH WENT TO THE TEMPLE TO PRAY" –

1. What is your reaction to today's media frenzy surrounding scandals?

2. How do you feel about public figures who are very outspoken about their faith?

3. Do you think this story (Luke 18:9–14) is as offensive to us today as it was to the church leaders in Jesus' day? Why or why not?

4. With whom do you identify the most in these verses? Explain.

   • The listeners "who were confident of their own righteousness and looked down on everyone else"
   • The Pharisee
   • The tax collector

5. What is your reaction to the welcome message in the bulletin at the Lady of Lourdes church? Would this message be a safe welcome in your church? Why or why not? How can church members be more welcoming to people who act, look, and believe differently?

6. How can one be more mindful of his or her true spiritual condition?

7. Unpack this statement from Jerry Bridges: "Your worst days are never so bad that you are beyond the reach of God's grace. And your best days are never so good that you are beyond the need of God's grace."

8. Share your one, big take-away from this chapter. How does this story (Luke 18:9–14) change the way you will live today? What is God's personal message for you in this story?

- STEPS TO CHRIST -

1. Which is dumber? To take seventy years and toss away eternity, or to take one year and chuck the seventy? Explain.

2. React to the idea that even if our ambitions for heaven begin with a purely selfish motivation—a heaven to win and a hell to shun—God will happily meet us where we are and work with our twisted motives.

3. Have you ever tried to fill a God-shaped vacuum with an addiction other than God? If so, how did that work out? What do you think is Satan's most effective substitute that people use in the place of god—alcohol, pornography, busyness, screen addictions, and so on?

4. Share the mental picture you have of God. Has this picture changed through the years? If so, how?

5. Is it your impression that Christians tend to focus on their "sins" (lying, cheating, stealing, etc.) or "sin" (not trusting God)? How does one's focus affect the overall satisfaction and success of his or her spiritual journey?

6. Share your reaction to this statement: "We are utterly hopeless but not worthless." How does this color your picture of God?

7. Describe the freedom that results from giving up the battle of fighting sins.

– KNOWING FOR SURE –

1. Is it possible to have a successful marriage without any communication? Explain.

2. In your opinion, what are the three most important components for a healthy, fulfilling, and intimate marriage? Would these components be the same for a healthy, fulfilling, and intimate connection with God? Why or why not?

3. What other metaphors besides marriage might help to describe one's relationship with God?

4. Read Ephesians 5:25–32. What role, if any, does the church play in helping people develop and nurture vibrant, personal relationships with Jesus?

5. Discuss this statement: "The couple that has been married for five minutes is just as married as the couple celebrating fifty-five years of marriage." What does this suggest about a Christian's assurance of salvation?

6. If a street preacher should corner you and shout the question, "Are you saved?" how would you respond and why?

7. Why do you think many people struggle with the assurance of salvation?

8. "Our behavior and our good deeds have nothing whatever to do with the reality of our salvation." Do you agree or disagree with this statement? Why? What about the corollary to this statement: "Our bad deeds, therefore, have nothing to do with causing us to be lost"?

9. Unpack the idea of willing obedience. When we disobey, does that affect our salvation? If so, how? Is all disobedience willing?

10. Is it a new idea to you that a person's certainty of salvation is directly related to an ongoing relationship? What does this mean for you in your own journey of faith?

- STEPS IN CHRIST -

1. To which character(s) in the parable of Ben Trying do you relate most closely and why?

2. Describe your experience with prayer. Did your prayer life change after you received Christ as your personal Friend and Savior? If so, how?

3. How does prayer as "communication for communication's sake" compare to the mind-set of viewing prayer as a vehicle to get what we want from God?

4. Discuss this statement: "Repentance is not so much something we do as it is something we can't help doing when we really come to Christ." Is this a new idea for you? How does it affect the way you understand repentance?

5. Read several different translations of 1 John 1:9. Note who it is who purifies us "from all unrighteousness." Is this an act of the human spirit or of the Holy Spirit?

6. Is it possible to have true obedience apart from a personal relationship with Jesus? Explain.

7. Share your thoughts about the idea of impulsive obedience. Have you experienced impulsive obedience? What is the key factor in the process of growing to the point of obeying out of impulse, rather than gritty determination or guilt?

8. Have you ever felt guilty about neglecting Christ's call to be an evangelist? Would you say an evangelist is more like a salesperson trying to sell God or a matchmaker trying to connect two friends? Explain.

– Spiritual Failure for Dummies –

1. What would you say is the primary reason for spiritual failure?

2. Looking at the downward spiritual spiral in Jehoshaphat's life, what do you think, based on your experience, is the best way to avoid each step of his fall? Which step tends to be your greatest struggle:

    - Going where you don't belong?
    - Listening to Satan's flatteries and entertaining the thought of compromise?
    - Refusing to obey the clearly revealed will of God?

3. Brainstorm some practical ways to let God fight the battle.

4. Reflect on Jehoshaphat's prayer: "I do not know what to do, but my eyes are upon You." When might this prayer be most useful? What's the best way to make this prayer habitual?

5. To which part of Jehoshaphat's story do you relate the most?

6. "You are good enough just the way you are for God to love you. But God loves you too much to let you stay the way you are." How do you feel about this statement? What does it say about the character of God?

7. Consider the idea that transformation happens by trusting, not trying. Which of the following would you say?

    - "This causes me to question whether or not transformation can really happen."
    - "I believe this in theory but have a hard time putting it into practice."
    - "I have seen this for others but not for myself."
    - "I have experienced this for myself."

- SICK FAITH VERSUS STRONG FAITH -

1. Have you heard Elder Venden's parable of the highway to heaven before? Share your reaction to the story. In what ways can you personally relate to the story? In what ways do you have a hard time relating?

2. Describe your best friend. How did you become best friends? How do our human friends inform our understanding of a friendship with Jesus? How are human friendships and our friendship with Jesus the same? How are they different?

3. Contrast the following Bible verses. Are these verses contradictory? How can we fight and yet yield the battle to God?

   • "Do not be afraid nor dismayed . . . for the battle is not yours, but God's" (2 Chronicles 20:15, NKJV).
   • "Fight the good fight of the faith" (1 Timothy 6:12, NKJV).

4. What does the story of the Canaanite woman (Matthew 15:21–28) reveal about Jesus? What does it tell us about people we might label as outcasts? When, if ever, have you acted like the woman? Like the disciples? Like Jesus? What's the big take-home from this story that you believe God wants to see happen in your life?

5. How would you define faith? Provide a picture of sick faith and strong faith.

6. Share a personal paraphrase of 1 John 2:1: "I write this to you so that you will not sin. But if anybody does sin, we have an advocate with the Father—Jesus Christ, the Righteous One" (NIV).

– GROWTH IN GRACE –

1. What is the biggest distraction in your spiritual life?

2. If we cannot grow by trying to grow, and we can grow only by eating, why is it so common for Christians to focus on growing rather than eating?

3. How might a person turn Bible study, prayer, and witnessing into a system of works as an attempt to earn salvation? What is the appropriate use of the spiritual disciplines in relation to one's salvation?

4. Using the analogy between the physical and spiritual life, add your own points to the following observations made in this chapter.

   • Invest the same amount of time to your devotions with Jesus as you spend eating meals.
   • Nobody can eat for you. You must consume the Living Bread for yourself.
   • Just as breakfast is the most important meal of the day, so it is wise to eat spiritually at the outset of every day.

5. How do you personalize your study of Scripture?

6. What suggestions do you have to enhance the two-way communication of prayer?

7. Share what the Lord means to you.

- GRAPE EXPECTATIONS -

1. On a scale of 0 (0 = not at all) to 10 (10 = very much), how are you affected by the thought that many church members are not really expected to grow spiritually? Explain.

2. How does this teaching about the vine fit into the broader discourse of John 14:15–16:16 about the work of, and our need for, the Holy Spirit?

3. Unpack this statement: "We are not called upon to produce the fruit, but simply to bear it."

4. What does it look like in real life for someone to "remain in Christ"? Be as specific as possible.

5. Share a time of God's pruning in your life. What did you learn? How did you change? What did God reveal about Himself to you during that time?

6. Do you see something in your life today that needs pruning? If so, what?

7. How does living with an awareness of God's presence change things? What practices might enhance that awareness?

8. Who comes to mind when you think of a person living in the Spirit? Why?

– Using Your Will –

1. Who comes to mind when you think of somebody with extraordinary willpower?

2. How would you answer the questions posed in this chapter? Are we transformed by faith plus effort? And if sanctification happens by faith alone, then what role does our will play in our relationship with God?

3. In the spiritual life, where is the real battle? And when Elder Venden speaks about where the battle *isn't*, what is he talking about? How does one stay focused on the true fight of faith?

4. Discuss the distinction between *will* and *willpower*. Do you agree or disagree with the contention that the *will* is one's power of choice, while *willpower* is the self-discipline and determination to do something? Explain.

5. Much discussion in the church has centered on the dangers of spiritual formation. On the one hand, doesn't Jesus want every one of His children to be formed into His likeness? On the other hand, is there not a danger of emptying one's mind and becoming vulnerable to the hypnotic dangers of Satan taking up residency? How does John 15:1–17 inform our understanding of spiritual formation?

6. What does "surrender" look like? Sound like? Feel like?

– VICTORY BY GRACE–OR GIMMICKS? –

1. Share a memorable victory in a contest—sports, music competition, spelling bee, whatever. Where were you? Why was it meaningful to you? What emotions did you feel?

2. What is your reaction to the suggestion that we should stop trying to do what's right and start training to build an intimate friendship with Jesus?

3. Does an emphasis on nurturing a friendship with Jesus potentially undermine spiritual victories? In other words, if—for the sake of beginning to know Jesus—you stop focusing on trying to do what's right, might there be an interim of anarchy? How do you feel about the way that Elder Venden addresses this concern? Do you agree or disagree? Why?

4. Place yourself on this continuum:

Weak willed (-10) _____ 0 _____ (10) Strong willed

5. React to the following statements:

   • "Relationship is its own biggest safeguard against license."
   • "The big divider between cheap righteousness by faith and the real deal is the devotional life."
   • "Surrender must embrace more than overcoming bad behaviors."

6. Share your favorite oxymoron. Do you think the term *partial surrender* is an oxymoron? Why or why not?

7. What gimmicks have you heard about that are used to assure spiritual victory and the overcoming temptation? How well do these approaches work for a strong-willed person? How well do they work for a weak-willed person?

8. How closely does the following quote mesh with your experience: "The secret to victory over temptation is to come before the throne of grace long before the temptation ever arrives and to know that close relationship and the constant dependence upon Jesus all the time."

– THE WHOLE SHEBANG IN THREE WORDS –

1. Share a story of decluttering in your life. How did the experience make you feel? Was it difficult? Do you tend to hoard, or get rid of stuff?

2. Why do you think most people are reticent to admit guilt?

3. Discuss the statement: "When it comes to righteousness, there's no difference between the serial killer and the saint."

4. How would you define *grace*?

5. Play a "word pop" game and have everyone shout out the first thing that comes to mind when he or she hears the following words:

   - sinner
   - forgiven
   - liar
   - punishment
   - stripes
   - healed
   - clean

6. What do these impulsive responses reveal about one's understanding of the gospel?

7. Is growth optional in a Christian's life? Why or why not?

8. If transformation does not occur by focusing on behavior modification, then how does it happen? Is it possible to be an authentic follower of Jesus without experiencing the modification of one's behavior? Explain.

9. Who comes to mind when you think about the gospel incarnated in a life? Why?